Whispers
of Love
in
Seasons
of Fear

Other Books by Terry Wardle

Draw Close to the Fire
Wounded
One to One
Exalt Him

Whispers of Love in Seasons of Fear

Terry Wardle

Chosen Books

A Division of Baker Book House Co
Grand Rapids, Michigan 49516

Published by Chosen Books
a division of Baker Book House Company
P.O. Box 6287, Grand Rapids, MI 49516-6287

Printed in the United States of America

Library of Congress Cataloging-in-Publication Data

Wardle, Terry.
    Whispers of love in seasons of fear / Terry Wardle.
    p. cm.
    Includes bibliographical references.
    ISBN 0-8007-9267-X (alk. paper)
    1. Peace of mind—Religious aspects—Christianity. 2. Fear—
Religious aspects—Christianity. I. Title.
BV4908.5.W37   1999
248.8p6—dc21   98-30480

For current information about all releases from Baker Book House,
visit our web site: http://www.bakerbooks.com

To my daughter Cara
Your love has brought healing to my life

Contents

Acknowledgments

Cheryl, my wife, and our son and two daughters, Aaron, Cara and Emily, have been an integral part of this book. They have walked this journey with me, offering encouragement and love along the way. Their acceptance and patience have been an important part of my life and of writing this book. I am grateful that in spite of my weaknesses, they have continued to believe in me even when others had their doubts.

Special friends like Sarah Herring, Patty Taylor and Peter Burgo contributed to this project with encouragement, suggestions, proofreading and technical support. Their affirmation and honest appraisal were invaluable to the completion of this book. Peter Kuiper, director of the New Life Clinic in Pueblo, Colorado, read the manuscript and provided insights into the battle with fear that helped me, not only as a writer but as a person on the journey to freedom and peace. I am grateful that Pete is my friend. Terry Klein, director of the New Life Clinic in Colorado Springs, helped me address my own fear issues and is one of the most gifted counselors I know.

Jane Campbell, my editor, has the gift of encouragement, as well as great skill and wisdom in the field of publishing. Working with her is a pleasure. Countless people at

Chosen work to make a book like this both readable and marketable.

To all these people, I say, Thank you! I really could not have done this without your help.

Some of the names and contexts shared in this book have been changed to protect some very special people.

The Journey Begins

The pilgrimage we will discuss in this book is one I have undertaken myself—the journey from fear to peace. From my earliest days I have struggled with seasons of fright and panic. Some of my most vivid memories from childhood are of periods of intense fear—unreasonable, for sure, yet painful and costly. As I grew I learned how to manage and even overcome my fears with effective coping mechanisms. But over the years the risks of life became more powerful than the childish techniques I had learned to control fear. As a result, by God's grace, I was forced into a season in which I had no choice but to look beyond the fear to the darkness that gave it life.

This process has taken time and exacted a high toll, at least by the world's standard of measurement. But whereas some may think I have lost, in fact I have found treasure beyond description. I have discovered Jesus' presence and strength in the midst of my own weakness. I have experienced transforming, patient love that has satisfied me as nothing else could.

I am not strong and courageous, as most would define these terms. I am not a superstar who has walked from victory to victory. I have met God most in the broken moments and disappointments of life. I write as one who has been healed and set free in many areas deep within and who has been overwhelmed repeatedly by the grace of His loving presence. I come to you as a man with battles yet to be won, wounds still in need of His touch and lies yet to be revealed and untwisted deep within my life. If you struggle with fear, know that I am a fellow traveler who desires to identify the landscape of this journey in a way that will help you see and experience Christ Jesus along the way.

Some have challenged the autobiographical flavor of my more recent books. I can respond only that Jesus has met me in the context of my own life. It is the place where His marvelous story has come alive for me. So it is that I share parts of my life journey as possible connecting points with you, hoping and praying that they will open your own heart to the healing power of our dear Lord.

I am fully convinced that the pilgrimages we make as individuals are not exclusively our own. They are in some mysterious, gracious way part of everyone's journey, and as such must be told. Not in a self-serving way that smacks of self-promotion! I pray that is not the feeling one gets from reading about my struggles. Rather, may they be relayed as part of the ageless testimony of God's grace made perfect in weakness and brokenness. As for me, I am a pilgrim walking with a limp as I seek to follow Him to higher ground than I could ever achieve apart from His benevolence and grace.

A Story of Fear

It was obvious to everyone in church that Sunday morning that Bill Henry was hurting deeply. The pastor had asked if anyone needed special prayer, and almost immediately Bill rose to his feet. Because the congregation was small, it was customary for people to share their requests openly. Individuals with needs would stand and explain why they wanted prayer, and then the pastor or an elder would lift the concern before the Lord. My family and I had attended the church enough to realize this was a regular part of their life together. But as Bill rose to his feet, his eyes watering and voice cracking, he awakened the body to an even greater level of concern.

I had heard about Bill for some years but had met him only the previous week. A leader in his denomination, concerned for world evangelization, he spent much of his time traveling around the world to encourage and support missionaries involved in frontline evangelism. Bill has a heart for God and for lost men, women and children throughout the world. He has given of his time, his resources, his very life for the work of the Lord, and countless people have been helped through his dedicated efforts. But on this Sunday morning it was obvious to everyone that Bill was the one who needed help.

It must have been hard for him to share his burden with us that day, but he pushed through the emotional storm to talk about his need. With head bowed and little eye contact with those around him, Bill confessed hesitantly that he was waging a battle with fear. For some time, he told us, he had been experiencing bouts of great fear, and at times attacks of panic. It was particularly bad when he was traveling, he said, especially when he felt closed in, such as on an airplane, in a crowd or in the back of a car. Bill described how his heart would race, his hands would get sweaty and he would experience a compelling desire to run.

As he talked, he actually began to weep. The church was silent as he told us, his voice breaking, how much he wanted to continue to serve the Lord yet was close to giving up his ministry because he could no longer handle the battle with fear.

It must have been difficult for Bill to open up, yet he was obviously desperate. On the one hand he struggled with shame, berating himself that a child of God, as long in the faith as he, would have such a problem. On the other hand he felt angry because he had sought the Lord's help repeatedly and memorized countless Scripture passages admonishing him to trust the Lord and not be afraid. But for whatever reason (certainly unknown to Bill), the battle continued. He had even gone so far as to seek deliverance, seemingly to no avail.

So here he was on a Sunday morning, reaching out to his brothers and sisters for understanding and support.

I detected fear in Bill's voice as he shared his story— rooted, I suspected, in concern over people's reactions. How would they respond to his confession? After all, he was known as a leader and Spirit-filled man of God. Would his fellow church members reject him as weak and hypocritical? Would they rebuke him, challenging his devotion with insensitive questions like "Where is your faith?" and "Don't you trust the Lord?" Would they try to quick-fix him with scriptural admonitions, all of which he had been attempting to follow? Or would they weep with him and accompany him before the Lord for direction and ultimate healing?

Thankfully Bill experienced only love and care from his friends that day. They had few answers, but they pointed him in prayer to the One who could help and meet him in that frightened place deep within his soul.

As I watched and listened, my heart was stirred for Bill and I knew he was not alone in his weakness. Countless men and women share a similar conflict with fear. I know, for I have been part of that number for a long, long time.

Many People Battle Fear

Many Christians—men and women who genuinely love the Lord and want to please Him in every way—fight fear. Some struggle silently, afraid to admit their problem for fear of rejection. Others, possibly more desperate and less proud, share the war within their lives, yet experience little relief or victory as a result of their openness. Many are greatly discomforted by fear, while others are disabled, at one level or another, by its destructive power. Many of these dear folks memorize appropriate Scripture, seek healing prayer, try the newest behavior modification techniques and, when really desperate, seek deliverance from evil spirits.

For some these wonderful channels of the Spirit's ministry do bring relief and, at times, freedom. But for many who battle fear, these activities do not seem to help. And after a while frustration, anger, shame and guilt take over to compound the dilemma all the more. The question they all ask is, Why?

Be assured, it is not because God's Word is not true. Nor is it that God fails to answer prayer, bring healing or set the evil one running in defeat. No, your heavenly Father is powerful, faithful and true. He is filled with great love and compassion toward all the hurting members of His family.

The issue is not God. When you experience little relief from the clutches of fear, there exists a deeper problem within you of which fear is but the symptom, not the cause. Pray about fear all you will; it never really addresses the core weakness within your life. Beneath the panic and paralyzing fright exists a dark place within your soul where untouched wounds, unmet needs, twisted beliefs and lies from the evil one abide. It is a frightening place, and as a result you simply do not want to go there—and naturally so! Addressing the fear seems the more logical and, frankly, easier route to freedom. But I assure you, it is not. The healing you need

15

regarding fear will occur in that seemingly forbidding place, and it will be the Lord who does the work, with you there to participate through surrender and trust.

I want to encourage you, then, to invite the Lord to do a work at the core of your life, where your deepest need is and where fear gains its disabling power. I assure you, He will meet you there with infinite tenderness and understanding. Although you might dread His anger or disapproval, I promise you that He will not come to you that way. His love for you is unfathomable and His patience unending. While the evil one would have you believe that the Lord is disappointed in you because of your struggle with fear, it is a lie. The Lord Christ wants to embrace you in the midst of weakness and pain and bring His glorious light to the dark places that represent strongholds of fear in your life. Jesus stands ready, with arms outstretched in love, to heal your wounds, to satisfy the unmet needs at the core of your life, to untwist the lies that have bound you and to give you His strength to face the risks and unknowns that are common to life on this side of God's Kingdom.

I do not suggest that He will give you an easy life with no chance of getting hurt, being rejected, facing a handicap or experiencing great loss. Such a place is yours in eternity, but not here on earth! What Jesus *will* do, if you allow Him, is bring you to rest and contentment deep within, in the very place where darkness once reigned. He will quicken you to experience His presence in the inner part of your being, and from there strengthen you to face life and its risks with new confidence and contentment.

The peace you experience will be based not on the calm of your circumstances but on the assurance that God is committed to good in your life and that, regardless of the situation, He will draw you ever close and conform you to the glorious likeness of Jesus.

16

I admit, getting to this place will not be without some discomfort. The Lord may, in fact, need to take you into a desert season with all your normal distractions and painkillers out of reach. But if He does, it will be motivated by His great love for you and His commitment to free you from the fears that have locked you in bondage.

Those who seek a problem-free world fail to see that peace is not a state conditioned by the absence of potential harm. It is, rather, the Presence that promises ultimate good. Ultimate good, in terms of the Kingdom, is found in knowing Jesus, in experiencing the joy of His embrace and in becoming like Him in love and holiness. These wonderful treasures are found not in a constant (and, I might add, futile) effort to avoid risk and pain, but in the continuous search for His presence even within the moment of trial and during the season of darkness.

If you make problem-free living your goal, you are reaching for something far inferior than God's best for you. He wants you to reach for Him just as He is reaching out to you, even in the midst of the fearsome, the risk-filled and the difficult. He yearns to show you the seeds of your fear and eliminate them from your life. He longs to have you participate with Him in digging up the very roots that feed and sustain their destructive power within your life. And in their place He desires to plant the seeds of His Spirit that will bring forth good fruit, able to sustain you and bring wholeness to your life.

It is my prayer that this book will help you go to the place where fear gains its strength, and eliminate, by Christ's presence, the very ground fear feeds on. It is not an exhaustive word on the battle with fear. But I do believe it is a word that will move you from fear to trust, from loneliness to union with your heavenly Father, and from anxiety to peace. While the battle with fear is mighty and often fought on many fronts, the Lord is infinitely greater and thoroughly committed to good things for your life. He will, if you surrender to the process, lead you to the very command center of fear in your life, dispel the darkness by His glorious light and there establish a stronghold of His strength and peace for your well-being.

That great work begins right now, with your own willingness to be open and vulnerable with Him.

Questions for Reflection and Review

1. What fears are you battling and how do they restrict your life?

2. What effect has your struggle with fear had on your self-image?

3. Do you feel like a weaker Christian because you battle fear? If so, why?

4. What response would you anticipate from others if you were to tell them about your struggles with fear?

5. Does that anticipated response keep you from sharing your problem? Why?

6. Have you memorized Scripture as a strategy against fear? Where has it helped and where has it not affected your struggle?

7. What is meant by the following statement from this chapter: "Beneath the panic and paralyzing fright exists a dark place within the soul where untouched wounds, unmet needs, twisted beliefs and lies from the evil one abide."

8. Is peace based on the absence of problems and risk or on the presence of God in the midst of life? Why do you believe this?

Vulnerability
Is the First Step

Is *vulnerability* a four-letter word for you? Does the notion of sharing your battle with fear make you nervous? Does the phrase *Be honest* cause you to think about punishment and rejection? Would it seem wrong of you to burden someone else with your problem? Does previous experience tell you that such openness does little to help and could even bring a great deal of hurt into an already difficult situation? Are you hesitant even to be honest before God, for fear of His rejection or rebuke?

For many people considering vulnerability, the answer to each of these questions is a resounding yes! Yet the first step to overcoming obsessive fear is choosing to be open and honest about your problem in a safe, supportive environment. But that first step will not be easy. The idea of sharing the details of your struggle can bring about more than a little discomfort. It can seem risky and in some ways wrong.

Why Don't We Like to Be Vulnerable?

Let's look briefly at some of the reasons we feel uncomfortable about being vulnerable and align them with the truth of God's Word.

"I Handle My Problems on My Own"

Many of us are hesitant about, or even opposed to, sharing our problems with others. One reason: We have been taught that the way to get through life is to be self-sufficient and self-reliant. After all, isn't that part of the very fabric of American society? Rugged individualism! Men in particular, it seems, buy into this notion and are closed about their struggles, whether with fear or other weaknesses. But the fruit of self-reliance is seldom good. What may begin as a small problem can, in secret, race out of control and eventually bring great bondage and destruction.

As I write this, my mind goes to Ken, who came to me at age 51 to admit he was in bondage to a sexual behavior that had begun in early adolescence. He had never shared it with anyone, and his silence had given the problem room to grow stronger. But his father had ingrained into Ken's mind that men do not discuss their problems with others; they just handle them. Unfortunately, this approach enabled the problem to handle Ken!

Countless passages in the Bible call you into the community of God's people, where you can receive and give help and support. One of my favorite Scriptures is this one in which the "Teacher" writes:

> There was a man all alone; he had neither son nor brother. There was no end to his toil. . . . Two are better

than one, because they have a good return for their work: If one falls down, his friend can help him up. But pity the man who falls and has no one to help him up! Also, if two lie down together, they will keep warm. But how can one keep warm alone?

Ecclesiastes 4:8–11

Being open and vulnerable with a few sensitive, caring brothers and sisters is perfectly in line with God's plan for your life. Such openness can be the doorway to freedom and can bring about a Spirit-empowered bonding that will strengthen you for the journey through fear to the Lord's lasting peace and strength.

"I Don't Want People to Think Less of Me"

First, let's face the truth. We live in a world where people—including at times some Christians—have not learned that condemning and judging others is wrong. As a result there are those who may hear of your struggle and possibly think less of you.

When I openly shared my battle with depression, there were a very few who did, in fact, say hurtful and insensitive things and who, as a result of my struggle, no longer felt comfortable under my ministry. To give the impression that openness never brings a negative reaction would be inaccurate. If this happens, tell the Lord how badly it hurts, receive His comfort and then move to be forgiving.

For many of us, however—possibly for you, too—the root of the matter is really pride. You simply do not want people to think you are weak or that you do not have everything all together in your life. You (like all of us) prefer people to see only the part of you that is solid and successful, not the place of fear and weakness. That this feeling is based in unhealthy self-protection and pride is obvious and without defense. Scripture is clear, moreover, that such

21

an attitude is not consistent with the way of the Kingdom and can lead to greater harm (see Proverbs 16:18).

God calls you to humble yourself toward Him and toward other Christians (see James 4:10; 1 Peter 5:6). Granted, this is not easy, but it is part of the Lord's pathway to wholeness for your life. Admitting your struggle with fear opens the way for God to touch you—through His people and also by the intimate presence of His Spirit deep within.

As I say this, I must also exhort you not to be unwise and simply tell anyone and everyone that you are battling fear in your life. That may invite rejection from some who are insensitive and condemning. Be vulnerable only with people who are safe and caring. (I will say more about this in a following section.) Know that while vulnerability is important to your ongoing growth and health, there is no need to expose yourself in a way that could hurt more than help.

"My Friends Have Enough Problems and I Don't Want to Burden Them"

Just yesterday I had the opportunity to spend some time with a nationally known Christian leader. We had lunch together to talk about a training seminar for some of his workers. In the midst of the conversation I told him I was writing a book on fear but felt somewhat hesitant about it because I am still on the journey toward freedom. He told me that he, too, battled fear, particularly regarding the well-being of his children. It went beyond concern, he said, to obsession.

For a while we talked about our common journeys, then went on to other topics. As we finished our lunch, we both commented that we felt better somehow about our struggles, even though we had not offered specific help or advice to one another. Although we both were burdened and busy, vulnerability had not increased our load but lightened it. Why? Because we had placed no unhealthy expectations on one another through sharing; we were simply committing support and care.

You can burden people with your problems, on the other hand, when one of three things is true. First, *if in telling them you expect them to be responsible to solve the dilemma and get you out to freedom.* This is an unhealthy expectation and the basis of very dysfunctional relationships. While you can ask others to support you on your journey to peace, they are not responsible to do the work on your behalf. Frankly, that is a formula for codependency. Being open with a few close people in your life is not a cry for them to fix you. It is a call for them to listen, love and lead you to the Lord, who can carry you out to freedom.

A second way you can burden others is *by being insensitive to their needs.* Some people are in a place of significant struggle themselves and may not be able to be there for you as much as you wish or even need. It is critical that you honor that fact and not put expectations on them that might hurt their own pilgrimages. There are times that those close to you are unable to give you anything more than the strength that comes through their common affection and love.

Third, we can burden others *when we ask them for a degree of direction and support beyond their gifting, anointing and experience.* I worked out some of the deeper personal issues of my own pilgrimage with a fine Christian counselor. My friends cared but had neither the background nor the gifting to help me through the tougher places. To have asked them for that level of support would have been unfair and could have been burdensome.

Approaching vulnerability with wisdom and sensitivity can be a marvelous opportunity to connect with others and experience the presence of the Lord. It can actually lessen the pressure of your struggle and enrich their lives as well. The admonition of Paul is the essence of what sharing one another's burdens is all about: "Rejoice with those who rejoice, weep with those who weep" (Romans 12:15, RSV). That is the heartbeat of vulnerability—a willingness to let others enter your struggle, with no greater expectation than that they hold you and show they care.

"I'm Afraid People Will Reject Me"

One of the battles I have fought in recent years has been a fear of flying. It has not been easy admitting it, and it makes me a bit uncomfortable revealing it here. But it is a place in my life in which the Lord has been doing a work.

For years I loved flying, first as a youth riding along with my dad in a Piper Cub, and then as an adult jetting across the United States to speak and teach. I found it relaxing and enjoyable.

But on a flight one day from Pittsburgh to Oklahoma, where I was to do a conference, I became paralyzed with panic. (I will talk later about why this happened.) Suffice it to say, I felt claustrophobic and wanted out of the airplane immediately. Overwhelming terror seized me and I actually thought I was going to pass out from sheer fright.

I made it to the ground, of course, but never wanted to fly again! Unfortunately it was a long walk from Tulsa to Pittsburgh, so I had to board another jet within a few days. I tried everything I knew to break this fear before the flight, to no avail. I was just as scared on the return trip, and I battled panic on every flight after that. I would fly when absolutely necessary, but I hated it.

I also wrestled with deep feelings of shame and humiliation, as you can imagine. After all, I was a Christian and a minister and should be afraid of nothing, let alone flying! For a long time I told no one but my wife, too afraid of the rejection I might get. I read books on flying, tried all sorts of self-help techniques, rehearsed all the statistics that confirmed the safety of flying, and fought to overcome this problem. No success. Every trip took an awful emotional toll, sometimes making me sick physically before, during and after the flight.

Finally I decided to share my fear with a friend who was my superior in ministry. I still remember the restaurant we were having lunch in and the meal I was eating, although this was well over a decade ago. After small talk I took the plunge and described what was going on with me. My friend listened intently, then exclaimed, "Terry, what's wrong? Are you afraid to go to heaven?" Stunned to silence, I felt like a faithless worm, a whimpering child, an immature weakling who could not keep up with the big boys. I remember little else of our lunch together, except wishing I could take back all I had said and hide it deep away again.

For a long time I talked about the matter with no one else. Yet the problem worsened. I needed help but was afraid to admit it for fear of a similar reaction.

Truthfully I was just as afraid to talk to the Lord about the problem, because I did not want to face what I thought would be His disappointment. So I kept silent and tried to manage on my own, through avoidance, denial or distraction. But all that hiddenness only played into the hand of the evil one, strengthening his grip on this area of my life. I found myself all alone in a dark and scary place, trying to pretend that everything would be fine, all the while hurting deeply—and facing sustained terror on trips.

You may be thinking, *If the first step to freedom is vulnerability, you're not convincing me that it's worth the risk!* Actually, I want to point up the critical difference between vulnerability and exposing yourself in an unhealthy way. What I did by not being careful to share with someone who would honor my struggle with tender compassion and understanding was lay myself open to more pain. In hind-

25

sight I realize this colleague never talked about his own life or pilgrimage. He was in many ways a wonderful Christian man whom, to this day, I admire and deeply respect. But conversations always revolved around the work of ministry. Probably he was closed to his own personal struggles and would naturally have been uncomfortable with mine.

Eventually, out of pure desperation, I decided to share my struggle with someone else. I was very, very careful, making sure to the best of my ability that this man could be trusted with my pain. I watched him around other people and listened as they talked about how he had helped them. I was careful to see if he was a man in touch with his own weaknesses and an admitted fellow traveler. Finally I asked him for time and laid out the entire story.

What a difference! Brad was sensitive, compassionate and supportive. I was able to tell him about my fears, and the shame and guilt I experienced as a result of my struggle. I described in great detail my feelings and frustrations, at times even weeping in front of him.

Brad helped me go beneath the flying problem to some of the roots of fear in my life. He was gentle in his questions and advice, all the while assuring me that there was no judgment or disappointment, either from him or from God. He comforted me and promised to help me as the Lord directed. Then, each time we met, he gave me direction to move ahead on the path to freedom.

Brad was the first person to walk alongside of me on the journey toward greater understanding and healing with respect to this problem with flying. Talking with him was my first step toward addressing the deep wounds empowering that fear and moving on toward greater well-being.

There are two very important points to all this. First, you cannot win by hiding and holding onto your problem alone. It simply will not work. The issue will continue to eat away at you and could broaden into other phobias and fears. So be open and honest with someone who will help you move beyond fear to God's peace. You must be vulnerable.

But second, be wise about who that someone else is. While I challenge you to be vulnerable, don't expose yourself to people who may hurt you through insensitivity, humiliation or judgment. You are under no obligation to lay out all the details of your problem to just anyone. Find someone who, like my friend Brad, is a wounded healer, sensitive to the pain you are facing and familiar with your path toward wholeness. Look for a person or community committed to helping others in an atmosphere of love, acceptance and understanding. Find Christian brothers and sisters who are gracious, patient and quick to embrace you with acceptance and affirmation regardless of the level of brokenness in your life.

Believe me, such an experience of shared life will itself bring healing to your fearful soul! My own friendship with Brad, and later with a few gracious and loving people in California, touched me where techniques and self-help could never even get close. Safe people who love as Christ loves are essential to our journey!

"The Lord Will Be Displeased with Me"

The Lord longs to help you and will embrace you without condemnation or judgment. I can assure you from my own journey into the dark that our Lord harbors a wondrous love for you and cares deeply about your struggle. Far from speaking words of rejection and disqualification, Jesus longs to meet you in this place of pain, to bring healing to your wounds and truth to the confused places deep within your life.

Do not be afraid, then, to open up to your heavenly Father. He delights in you and sees far beyond your brokenness to the wonder of who you are in His Son, Jesus

Christ. The thought of His disapproval and rejection, although often perpetuated by the legalistic and religious among us, is birthed in hell itself. God loves you with a passionate, indescribable love. In Ephesians 3:18 Paul wrote that Christ's love is wider, longer, higher and deeper than you can ever fathom. Soaking in that love is precisely what combats the roots of fear (as we will discuss later). Opening up to His love through honesty and vulnerability will transform you from fearful to full of peace, from lonely in the battle to contented in His sweet embrace.

My friend Jay was once trapped in a destructive homosexual lifestyle. By God's grace he came to saving faith and has walked free for years. Some time later, however, I learned that Jay never enjoyed intimacy with the Lord. He served the Lord faithfully, even sacrificially. But nearness and vulnerability were not part of his life with God.

I found this out by accident while leading a prayer retreat that Jay attended. I was teaching about centering prayer and encouraging the group through an exercise to get quiet and ask the Father how He felt about them personally. I noticed that Jay almost came unglued! So while the others continued the exercise, we went off to talk. Jay told me he could not ask God how He felt about him because he feared the answer. Jay was convinced he would encounter nothing but disapproval and disgust. That fear had driven him to a frantic pace of service, hoping somehow he could win God's favor.

What a twofold deception of the evil one! First, that God would be angry and full of rejection for one of His children. The Lord Christ has paid the price for all our sins and received the full punishment on Calvary. As such every believer—including me, Jay and you—is heir to the riches of the Kingdom, with God's delight and embrace as the treasure above all others. Reread the story of the Prodigal Son in Luke 15 and you will see that God is not about rejecting and punishing His children, but about displaying great delight and love toward them, regardless of failure—past, present or future. That is why they call it Good News!

The second deception in Jay's thinking was that any level of performance and service could affect the Lord's love and embrace. This walk with God is all about grace. Service is a response to His great love, not a precondition. Nothing you did brought you His love and nothing you do can take it away. It is a gift, received and sustained in your heart by faith.

Your struggle with fear is not news to God and will not initiate rejection or punishment from Him. Go to Him and be honest and vulnerable about your problem. When you do, you will find a level of love that will empower you to walk on into the dark place where fear gets its power and life. The Lord will go there with you and bring you to new understanding and strength. He cares deeply about you and wants to help. Go to Him in the midst of your pain and be honest. There is no length to which He will not go to see you made whole.

In the next chapter we will look further at the matchless love of God and His deep concern for your well-being.

Questions for Reflection and Review

1. What feelings do you have when you consider sharing your struggle over fear with another person?

2. Have you ever had a negative experience while being vulnerable? What effect did that have on your willingness to be open with others?

3. Do you tend to try to handle problems on your own, and if so, why?

4. When, according to what you read in this chapter, is sharing with a friend problematic for you, and when can it be helpful?

5. Reread the story of my encounter with Brad. What made that a safe and helpful context for me to deal with my problem?

6. Where could you possibly turn for help and know it was a safe place for you to deal with your fear?

7. What would be important to know about a person with whom you were going to be vulnerable?

8. How does God look at you in light of your struggle with fear? Is that belief consistent with Scripture?

9. Is God's love for you conditional? How does He respond to weakness and failure in your life?

10. Jay tried to gain God's love through performance and service. What is wrong with that kind of relationship with God?

11. Why are openness and vulnerability critical to your healing?

God Is with You All the Way!

An experience I had several years ago has transformed my understanding of God's love and His commitment to the broken and weak. It gave me such a revealing glimpse into God's tender care that I have been encouraged to be open and vulnerable with Him about my own battle with fear. This insight came while I was involved at Spring Meadow in the mountains of Northern California (one of the most beautiful places on earth!) in an important ministry to broken men and women.

The ministry offered a variety of programs, including intensive retreats for small groups of hurting people. We would spend time together teaching, praying, fellowshiping and working on deep issues of brokenness. It became a tradition to break on the third day and visit Lassen National Park a few miles away. There we enjoyed leisure time to walk around Manzanita Lake at the base of the Lassen Volcano.

It was peaceful and beautiful there, perfect for refreshing us after hard work on personal issues. We always had lunch together beside the lake before going off for a time of solitude. As we sat by the shore eating, we would throw food to the ducks in the water. As soon as we approached the edge of the lake, the ducks would paddle up, quacking and begging for a treat. Everyone loved it, including our staff.

One day we saw among the waterfowl one small and tattered duck with a twisted, broken beak. He was jostled and pushed out of the way by the healthy ones, and when he got too near, the others attacked him and chased him away. Our entire group took up the cause of that wounded duck! Again and again we chased away the aggressive ducks, throwing food to the one with the twisted bill and treating him with more attention than we did the rest.

Each time we went to the lake that summer, the staff looked for that duck and paid him special attention. As a result he grew increasingly brave and would come out of the water, waddling right up to us. At times he ventured onto our blankets and even ate out of our hands. None of the other ducks received such care, nor did they ever get that close.

One day as we were giving morsels of bread to the tattered duck with the broken, twisted beak, I became overwhelmed with emotion. It was, for me, one of the window experiences described in my favorite book by Ken Gire, an inspired and gifted author. In this book, *Windows of the Soul*, Gire encourages his readers to look for God in everyday encounters with other people, with work, play, art, dreams, movies and the world of nature around us. He details how each of these can become, if your eyes are tuned in to them, a parable of God's activity—windows that will enable you to see beyond the obvious to the God who is there, always present.

At the lake in Lassen National Park, a window opened and I was looking beyond the pageant of the duck to the love of God for broken people and to the drama of the incarnation of Christ. I was so moved that everything seemed to stop in time, and I saw and felt the love of God for me and all these other broken, weak people as never before.

Three truths soaked into my soul that day that have opened me to vulnerability to God as nothing else ever has.

God Loves Broken People and Longs to Help Them

There we were, concerned about a weak duck with a broken bill. How much more does your heavenly Father care about you, especially when you are in deep pain, vulnerable to attack and scared of what life has brought your way? He is not put off by your problem with fear, lavishing all His attention on the whole, the strong and the beautiful while ignoring you. He picks you right out of the crowd when you are down and broken, placing far more attention on your needs than you could ever imagine.

That day at the lake I saw how attracted everyone was to the unhealthy duck and the care they gave it. God looks at broken people the same way, I realized, but with infinitely more concern and compassion.

Your struggle with fear moves the heart of God. He sees you and wants to help in every good way possible, if you will allow Him. Draw near and experience the power of His tenderness and warm, wonderful embrace. Scripture resounds with the truth of God's love for the weak, the broken and the fearful. Consider these verses that reveal that great love:

> The LORD is close to the brokenhearted and saves those who are crushed in spirit.
> Psalm 34:18

> [God] tends his flock like a shepherd: He gathers the lambs in his arms and carries them close to his heart.
> Isaiah 40:11

33

> "You are my servant; I have chosen you and have not rejected you. So do not fear, for I am with you; do not be dismayed, for I am your God. I will strengthen you and help you; I will uphold you with my righteous right hand."
>
> Isaiah 41:9–10

> A bruised reed he will not break, and a smoldering wick he will not snuff out.
>
> Isaiah 42:3

> "I live in a high and holy place, but also with him who is contrite and lowly in spirit, to revive the spirit of the lowly and to revive the heart of the contrite."
>
> Isaiah 57:15

> "I myself will tend my sheep and have them lie down, declares the Sovereign LORD. I will search for the lost and bring back the strays. I will bind up the injured and strengthen the weak. . . ."
>
> Ezekiel 34:15–16

These Scriptures are but a small representation of those that speak of God's heart for you, even when you are battling brokenness and fear. Your heavenly Father is not repulsed or disappointed by you, nor is He looking past you to all your healthy and whole brothers and sisters. He is longing for you to draw near that He might touch you and bring you freedom and strength.

The Father Has Gone to Great Lengths to Help You

There we were, throwing pieces of bread to a wounded duck and enticing him onto our blankets where we could feed him and protect him from attacks from the strong and healthy. Caring? Yes, we were all touched by his plight.

Costly? Hardly! None of us starved because we gave him a little of our lunch, and not one of us ventured into the water to give the little guy a hand. Passing on plunging into his watery world, we lured him instead onto our turf.

Does God have concern and love for the lost and broken? Nothing reveals the answer more than the incarnation of Christ. Your heavenly Father cares so much about your brokenness that He sent His Son, Jesus, to enter your world. He did not establish a royal throne on earth where you had to go for an audience and appeal for mercy. No, God's love is demonstrated in that He gave His only Son so you could be free. Jesus, as Paul wrote,

> made himself nothing, taking the very nature of a servant, being made in human likeness. . . . He humbled himself and became obedient to death—even death on a cross!
>
> Philippians 2:7–8

God's love and commitment for the broken and lost caused Him to act in the most radical way! He arranged to pay for your sin, heal your broken life and embrace you as His precious child. He made a way, through the broken body and shed blood of Christ, for you to come into His presence and receive strength and peace in the most trying of times. The narratives of the Lord's ministry here on earth demonstrate God's great concern for the weak and weary. Just read the stories of the Gadarene demoniac, blind Bartimaeus, the woman caught in adultery, the ten lepers, the woman at the well, Zacchaeus, the resurrection of Lazarus and the thief on the cross. All these accounts and many more point to one great truth: *God longs to embrace you in your struggle, even when it is costly!* That is the kind of love you can trust.

One of the most tender and moving stories in the New Testament is found in John 13. Jesus was soon to be betrayed by Judas, followed by His arrest, trial and crucifixion. Knowing the time was near, the Lord gathered with

35

His disciples for a final meal. After sharing the Last Supper, Jesus did something shocking. As John tells us,

> Jesus knew that the Father had put all things under his power, and that he had come from God and was returning to God; so he got up from the meal, took off his outer clothing, and wrapped a towel around his waist. After that, he poured water into a basin and began to wash his disciples' feet, drying them with the towel that was wrapped around him.
>
> verses 3–5

Jesus, the Son of God, humbled himself before mere men and knelt to wash their feet. It was an act of sacrificial service unknown and unexplainable to everyone present. Why did He do it? What moved Christ to stoop to such a meek position and wash the disciples' feet? The answer is found in the narrative:

> Jesus knew that the time had come for him to leave this world and go to the Father. Having loved his own who were in the world, he now showed them the full extent of his love.
>
> verse 1

Love and care for His own led the Lord to serve them in the most humble and tender way.

Jesus loves you with that same yearning love. He delights in you as His own and will meet you in the weak or broken places in your life where fear abides. Jesus not only died for you two thousand years ago, but He will also serve you in love in the hour of your distress today.

Openness Is the Doorway to God's Touch

Watching a duck with a broken beak can teach you a great deal. As I looked through the window of that living parable, I realized once again how upside down and backwards we have things—not only in the pagan world but within the Church as well. We are committed to appearing together, strong and healthy because we think it is the successful, the powerful, the rich and the famous who have it best. So we work hard to hide all our blemishes and faults in order to be noticed and accepted by those around us. Admit brokenness? Not on your life! That could be the sure prescription for rejection.

For years I worked hard to be accepted, performing to the best of my abilities, appearing strong, together and healthy. I had put all my frailties as far out of sight as possible and spent my time among the successful and popular. One day, however, the pressure of all that pretense brought me to my knees. I took off my mask before the people I was serving and told them I was not a superstar who had overcome all his problems but a broken, wounded man learning to be honest with God—a bird with a twisted, broken bill. I spoke openly about my battle with depression and my lifelong struggle to overcome fear in my life. I admitted that I was neither strong nor courageous in myself, but was finally willing to get the help I had needed for a long time.

Some gasped. Many others listened as I told them of my experience with God once the mask came off. I shared how tenderly He had touched me, drawn me into His arms and whispered the most endearing words of love. I talked with them about His delight and pleasure with me, even in my horrible condition of brokenness. I gave testimony to the fact that there is something far more important than being healthy, strong and successful. There is the opportunity to be intimate with God, who loves as no other.

As I shared those truths, an amazing thing took place. Countless friends who had appeared to be all together started taking off their masks and revealing broken, twisted beaks! They became real, realizing that with God it is O.K. to be honest and vulnerable about struggles. They began to go to Him in weakness and discover His strength and power. They started to admit their loneliness and fear, discovering the truth that God is always there with them, longing for sweet communion and intimate embrace.

In the Sermon on the Mount Jesus turned the value system of this world upside down, and then said this is what the Kingdom of God is like. In Matthew 5 we read these words of Jesus:

> "Blessed are the poor in spirit, for theirs is the kingdom of heaven.
> "Blessed are those who mourn, for they will be comforted.
> "Blessed are the meek, for they will inherit the earth.
> "Blessed are those who hunger and thirst for righteousness, for they will be filled.
> "Blessed are the merciful, for they will be shown mercy.
> "Blessed are the pure in heart, for they will see God.
> "Blessed are the peacemakers, for they will be called sons of God.
> "Blessed are those who are persecuted because of righteousness, for theirs is the kingdom of heaven."
>
> verses 3–10

Our Lord essentially said, "Happy are those who have twisted, broken beaks!" Why? Because they are very close to the Kingdom. Their weakness will drive them to God, and there they will experience a love that will change their lives forever. Astounding!

I have spent enough time with Christian leaders to know that there are a lot of hurting people serving the Lord who are afraid to admit their weaknesses. What a tragedy! Not only does this keep them in bondage and hinder their relationship with God, but it creates a false standard of Christian discipleship that sends the broken under their care into hiding. The average believer thinks leaders have it all together, and as a result tucks away his own problems and puts on his pretty mask. The truth is, we are all broken, and it is precisely in the place of weakness that God meets us with grace and makes us strong in Him. Paul's words in 2 Corinthians 12:9–10 support this reality:

> But he said to me, "My grace is sufficient for you, for my power is made perfect in weakness." Therefore I will boast all the more gladly about my weaknesses, so that Christ's power may rest on me. That is why, for Christ's sake, I delight in weaknesses, in insults, in hardships, in persecutions, in difficulties. For when I am weak, then I am strong.

If you want to experience healing in the dark place that empowers fear, be vulnerable with God and admit your weakness. Take off your mask and reveal to Him the twisted, broken part of you that needs His touch. He will meet you there in great tenderness and love and embrace you in arms strong enough to carry you through. Far from rejecting you, your heavenly Father will draw you close to His heart and whisper words of love that will drive away the fear.

Questions for Reflection and Review

1. What is a "window of the soul"?

2. Why were the people so drawn to the duck with the twisted bill?

3. Read the Scriptures found on pp. 33–34. What do they tell you about God's attitude toward the broken?

4. What does the incarnation tell you about God's heart for you?

5. Read the story of Jesus washing the disciples' feet found in John 13. Why was Jesus eager to serve them in this way?

6. What effect does our society's preoccupation with outer beauty and strength have on your willingness to be open about your struggles and weaknesses?

7. Did Jesus' teaching in the Sermon on the Mount complement or contradict the notion that brokenness is a curse to your life?

8. The Beatitudes could be titled "Happy are the Unhappy!" Why?

9. I wrote that revealing my "twisted beak" enabled other people to be open about their own struggles. Why do you think it had that effect?

10. What is the nature of your twisted beak?

Moving toward the Dark Place Where Fear Lives

Before we get any farther, it is important to recognize something about fear: It is not all bad! I would not want to live my life without the ability to experience fear at the appropriate time. It is a God-given physical and emotional response to potential danger that actually helps us tremendously. We were created to respond instantaneously when threat or danger presents itself.

Imagine that you are walking on the path at your favorite park. You are enjoying the warm day, the bright sunshine and the beauty of the flowers and trees. Happily you stroll along, feeling a settled peace and contentment. Suddenly, glancing to the side of the path, you see a rattlesnake coiled beneath a fallen log ten feet away. What happens? Instantly your brain registers danger, sending a signal to your adrenal glands. They respond by pumping adrenaline into your heart, which begins to race, and you feel compelled to move quickly out of danger. Better said, you turn around and run like the wind without looking back! This reaction is called the flight-or-fight response and actually serves an important role in protecting you.

In describing your feelings to someone else later, you would most likely say that you were afraid. But there is no problem with that, is there? You would not need counseling or inner healing prayer or a deliverance session to combat these feelings. They are natural and good and accomplish the job God intended. Fear in this case is both healthy and good.

But now, taking the same situation, consider the following. Having confronted the snake along the path and moved out of danger, what if now you refused ever to go to that park again? Not only that, but you decided not to allow your children to play in the yard, and you told their teacher that they were not permitted to go outdoors at recess. Every time you opened the front door, you were frightened that a snake might slither in, so you stood guard when someone came to visit, anxious that they get in quickly so you could bar the path of any reptilian intruder. You thought constantly of all possible snake encounters, and as you pondered them, fear and anxiety welled up to overwhelm you.

Now fear would no longer be your friend, would it? It would have become an enemy keeping you in bondage.

This kind of irrational and unreasonable fear, the kind that disables and debilitates, needs the attention of the Lord. It is the focus of our concern in this book and where we will now journey in order to find freedom and peace.

There are as many anecdotes and illustrations of fear as there are people on earth. Everyone has those scary places in their lives where irrational and obsessive fear reigns. As such I will not try to share multiple stories that may come close to the specifics of your own struggle. I do want to tell one person's story, however, which I believe illustrates the essential pattern present in all our battles with fear and panic.

The Anatomy of Destructive Fear

My wife, Cheryl, and I met David and Summer while we were serving at Alliance Theological Seminary in Nyack, New York. I was on staff as a professor there and David worked as a state police officer assigned to the West Nyack barracks. We first became friends through the local church and soon began spending some time together.

It did not take long to discover that Summer was driven by fear deep within in her life. A very religious person, she was forever in God's Word finding truth and memorizing Scripture passages. My first impression was that she was doing this out of pure delight for the Lord and His promises. But over time it became clear to me that even there, fear was driving her. In fact, it seemed that there was hardly an area where fear did not have her in a stranglehold.

David and Summer had two small children, Rachel and Robert, both beautiful and full of life. When we first met David and Summer, the kids were only two and five. Summer was forever fussing and fretting over them. She refused to allow them to go into the nursery at church. Why? For one thing, she was convinced that the workers did not police the toys well enough to keep her children from playing with things touched by kids under the weather. She was also concerned about people serving in the nursery who might possibly abuse Rachel and Robert. Even though the church was very careful about training and background checks, for Summer the risk was unacceptable. So the children went to church with Dave and her, and if they fussed, she took them out to an unoccupied room and watched them herself.

It was virtually impossible for Cheryl and me to go to dinner with David and Summer without their kids because Summer did not trust babysitters. On the rare occasions when they did leave the children with a sitter, she phoned home continually to see if everything was O.K. She did the same, I learned, when she put the kids to bed at night, checking and rechecking on them as they slept.

This behavior was focused not only on the children. Summer was forever checking on David at work, to the point of embarrassing him and putting his job at risk.

Summer permitted no junk food in the house and monitored all foods for any ingredients she felt might lead to cancer or some other illness. She was just as diligent about friendships. She would play over in her mind conversations she had had with friends. If she had said anything with the potential for being misunderstood, even obscurely, she would be on the telephone to make sure it was not taken to that conclusion. She fretted over, worked and managed friendships so that no one would be upset with her, even when there was absolutely no reason. The truth is, at times Summer drove friends away with this behavior, and even though she was told that her actions had this effect on people, she continued obsessively.

Summer had a list of rules that were just as oppressive, yet the suggestion that she adjust them sent her into a panic. She refused to eat in restaurants that served alcohol because she feared causing a brother or sister to stumble and then being judged by God for it. She would never be seen talking alone to a man, even in a crowd of Christians, because she did not want anyone to get the impression that she was not totally devoted to David. Summer would not go to movies because she feared their opening her mind to forces that would lead her astray and into sin. And if she and David were going on a trip, she had all her friends pray for safe travel, and while she was gone she would worry about the house, the money they were spending and the accidents they might incur along the way.

Some years after leaving Nyack, Cheryl and I were temporarily reconnected with David and Summer. Finally David had said he had had enough and demanded that Summer address these irrational and obsessive fears. She agreed, so long as she could begin the journey with Cheryl and me. Because we were involved in a spiritual direction and counseling ministry at the time, we agreed to help Summer at least to get started, knowing she would eventually need support beyond what we could offer.

It was in this context that I was able to discover what lay beneath the behavior that kept fear alive and active in her life.

What Are the Behavior Patterns?

Before considering the core wounds that had set up Summer's struggle with fear, let's consider the patterns of behavior that can be identified in her life. While your problem with fear may not be as broad or deep, the dynamics are virtually the same. I know they are in my life, and they can be as recognizable in my responses to risk as they are in the story of Summer.

Anticipatory Anxiety

As with most negative emotions, not all anxiety is bad. When I am asked to speak, I experience mild anxiety that serves me well. It motivates me to prepare and anticipate the moment in a way that makes my talk more effective.

When you are battling fear, however, anxiety begins to race out of control. Your mind begins to ponder each and every possible scenario of disaster, keeping you in a chronic condition of nervous irritation and fear. The "what-ifs" take over and drive you to respond in a dysfunctional and destructive way.

Consider one of Summer's anxieties. There is a degree of risk, of course, in placing your children in the care of a babysitter or nursery worker. When anxiety is serving properly, it leads a parent to check everything out to make sure things go well. That is not a problem; it is responsible behavior. But when the degree of anxiety and concern extends as far as it did with Summer, it is irrational, far out of proportion to the degree of risk.

With anticipatory anxiety, the mind goes far beyond concern, concocting every imaginable catastrophe and superimposing it onto the present moment. As I battled the fear of flying, for example, I reworked scenes of disaster over and over in my mind, even though the level of risk was far less than my level of concern. And, as with Summer and most who battle fear, it led to very unhealthy responses.

Control

What was Summer's response to her obsessive anxiety about the children in church? She insisted that she be in control. To calm her pain, which was the fear of harm to her kids, Summer took control and watched them herself.

Granted, there are many times in life when we are responsible and the one in control. But with irrational fear, you come to believe that only you are safe and that things will be all right only if you are the one controlling the situation. There are a host of ways people do this, including manipulation, aggression, avoidance and deception.

Regardless of the behavior, your goal is to avoid harm, whatever that means in the circumstance (for example, loss, rejection, ridicule, physical hurt or death). You do that by insisting that you and you alone hold the rudder and guide the craft safely to shore. Whether that response came because you were instructed that you were alone responsible or whether an event taught you that if someone else took charge you would be hurt, the behavior is the same: "If there's any degree of risk, I have to be in charge!"

Obsessive-Compulsive Behavior

The psychological disorder with this name involves (in lay terms) repeated irrational behaviors that a person performs obsessively in an effort to address inner turmoil and unrest. A classic example is the person who washes his or her hands over and over again, so much that it interferes with work and relationships and prevents normal function. I am not suggesting that someone who battles fear qualifies for this diagnosis. Not at all! I do believe, however, that most people who are trapped in fear have certain elements of this condition, even though it is not necessarily classifiable as a psychological disorder.

I have certain tendencies toward obsession myself. In some places in my life it has not been entirely bad. In fact, it has helped me fulfill goals and accomplish some good things in my life. But in other places it has been a real problem. There was a time, for example, when I battled agoraphobia quite severely, following a long season of depression.

Agoraphobia is a condition in which a person has acquired a large number of phobias and, as a result, becomes immobilized, to the point that he or she does not want to leave the house. Fearful of panic attacks, particularly in crowded places like restaurants and shopping malls, the individual retreats into an isolated existence in an effort to find safety.

In my own season of emotional upheaval, one particular phobia I developed was that of dying of a heart attack. Sudden panic attacks would send my heart racing, and each time I wondered if I was having a coronary episode.

During a regular checkup right in the middle of my struggle with agoraphobia, the technician giving me an

EKG asked if I had, in fact, recently had a heart attack. The reading, she told me, was suggesting that possibility. She fiddled with connections, looked concerned and made comments that almost sent me into cardiac arrest right there! Although all indicators turned out to be contrary, I began to obsess on that possibility. I thought about it day and night, and as I did I got very anxious and afraid. To address my discomfort, I read about the heart, began to jog, watched my eating and monitored my pulse and blood pressure regularly.

These can be normal and advisable activities. But what drove my behavior was obsessive and irrational fear. I was not washing my hands or counting out loud or engaging in any other obviously dysfunctional response. But I was acting out compulsively all the same in order to manage my fear.

Summer was doing the same thing, checking on the children obsessively, calling friends to see if they still liked her and watching foods like a soldier on guard duty in a war zone. These behaviors were driven by fear and aimed at reducing her discomfort.

The more you manage fear that way, the more power it gains. Instead of killing the fear, it gives it the dark attention it desires and feeds it to greater life.

Avoidance

"When all else fails, just avoid what you're afraid of doing." That could be a motto for many people who battle irrational and obsessive fear.

"If the degree of risk cannot be reduced by your control, or if the situation is such that you are powerless to address the risk, then just avoid placing yourself in that position." Again, this advice may sound reasonable, and it can temporarily eliminate the nagging pain of chronic fear attached to an event. But in the long run, avoidance can create disaster much deeper and far more problematic than most people anticipate.

I went years without significantly battling fear. But following a serious bout with depression, I began to experience panic attacks. In a particular situation I would suddenly feel my heart racing and experience the urge to run away from danger, even when there was none. Getting away did reduce the anxiety and help me feel peaceful again. So I began to avoid those places where such attacks occurred. But soon I was avoiding far too many places and activities and my fear level was only increasing. I was addressing panic and fear in an entirely wrong way, and it only strengthened the fear and reduced my world. Avoidance was working against me.

Granted, there are times you should avoid a situation. If there is an area near you where gangs and drive-by shootings occur regularly, you are wise not to take that route with your family on your way home from the mall. There is no problem in this kind of avoidance. But when irrational fear, such as in the fictitious snake tale at the beginning of this chapter, leads you to avoidance behavior, it is unhealthy.

I recognize, of course, that fear wears you down and you desire peace. But running is not the lasting answer. Neither is the opposite response healthy—obsessively facing the fear in order to prove to yourself that it will not rule you. I have a friend who grew fearful of bridges and crossed one near his home repeatedly in order to manage the fear and prove he could beat it. As with many of the responses we make to handle fear, that does not cut to the core of the problem.

Getting to the core is the only lasting answer.

Moving Deeper toward the Core Issues

You may be thinking, "Aren't there specific passages in God's Word that address all these issues?" Yes, there are.

49

And God's Word is powerful and capable of setting people free. I am all for memorizing the promises and directives of Scripture and using them in your battle against irrational and obsessive fear. But freedom comes when the truth of God is applied specifically to the problem being addressed. A passage of Scripture, true as it is, will accomplish little if it is not relevant to the real problem at hand. Ben-Gay is great for sore muscles, but apply it to hemorrhoids and you will not find it all that helpful! God's Word applied specifically will bring life, but confessing, "Fear not!" will not significantly help heal the wound that gives birth to your fear.

Take Summer. She was amazingly knowledgeable about the Bible and had memorized many specific texts relating to fear. But no matter how much she confessed them, they did not help. Why? Not simply because her knowledge of Scripture was mere head knowledge. She had a personal relationship with the Lord and a genuine passion to know Him better. But in her struggle with fear, the real battle went far deeper than fear itself. There were issues and hurts in her life that needed the Lord's transforming work. And confessing, "Fear not!" did not touch her core wounding that fear fed on. The power of God's Word and presence were required to heal, beneath the symptoms, the very core and cause of the struggle.

The same is true for you. Your battle goes deeper than fear to a place of darkness deep within your being. The Lord wants to minister freedom there, transforming that place of pain into an interior castle where He reigns, gives you strength and embraces you in love.

You will find that repeatedly I use the phrase *core wounding* in this book. I will unfold more on this theme throughout, but let me define my use of this central concept.

People everywhere, I am convinced, battle a sense of abandonment and loneliness deep within their lives, which generates a frightening darkness. So frightening, in fact, that they will do almost anything to avoid those debilitating feelings. This problem is the result of an inner wound experienced at the earliest stages of life, a byproduct of being separated from God. He is to be the source of love, acceptance, safety and security for all of us. But the Fall brought with it a disconnection from that source and a resulting sense of abandonment and loneliness.

This wound common to humanity is compounded when parents and significant others send messages of rejection and withdrawal, either intentionally or inadvertently, that threaten a child's sense of safety and well-being. The child perceives that he or she will be left alone when he fails or doesn't measure up, leaving him without the means to have his deepest needs met. This deep wound empowers all kinds of dysfunctional behaviors and distortions, including the battle with fear that we are exploring in this book.

Addressing the core issues that feed fear is no quick fix. If that is what you are after, what I am recommending will not meet your expectation. Lasting change is a process that takes time and involves work on your part. The journey to freedom also involves the Lord, whose work in your life will not occur according to some set prescription or schedule. He moves at the proper time and in the way He knows is best. Your role is to be open and honest and faithful to do your part. In essence you do the possible, as He directs, and He will do the impossible.

You may be thinking, "How long will this take?" If you mean how long until you experience total freedom, I cannot even guess. I have been on this journey for several years and have still more ground to cover. But this I do know: Lasting change happens by no other path. And along the way you will experience ongoing freedom that will bring you joy and keep you moving forward. Best of all, you will be growing ever closer to your Lord and feeling His love as never before! All that makes the journey worth taking, wouldn't you say?

Deep Wounds, Deep Brokenness

Like all of us who struggle with irrational fear, regardless of the breadth and severity, Summer had a deep wound that empowered her struggle. Having spent time counseling her, I was able to learn the specific dynamics of her core brokenness.

By considering Summer's story, I believe you will be able to discern some of the components of your own issues. While the actual circumstances and wounding events will be different, you will see into your own place of darkness and pain and, from there, be able to move ahead to specific steps that will enhance healing and freedom.

Far beneath the irrational fear and compulsive behavior in Summer's life was a dark and scary reality for her. She was not all that in touch with it, having locked it off from her conscious mind as a small child. She managed to do that through a variety of painkillers and distractions, much as you and I have. But the frightening place was there just the same—a virtual breeding ground for the fear and anxiety that kept her in a perpetual emotional stew.

Summer had been wounded severely and significantly in the earliest stages of her developmental life, and all that followed was a response to that reality. She came from an extremely dysfunctional family and was required to be responsible at a very early age for her parents' well-being. During their separation and eventual divorce, both parents played her against each other, though she was only eight years old, to get what they wanted. Her dad went so far as to tell Summer that if she chose to live with him, her mother would not divorce him. This message reinforced her feelings that safety and security were hers to maintain and control.

Part of Summer's desperation was the result of the Fall, as it is for all of us. Created to be one with the very source of her identity and security, she joined the human race only to experience a disconnection that was never meant to be. God intends, of course, that harmony with Him will bring an intimate knowledge that all of us are deeply loved and can face life with confidence from that center of being. The Fall severed that divine tie, however, and Summer, like every other person born to woman, felt the impact. Something critical was missing—or, rather, Someone. Compounding this emptiness was her experience at home only reinforcing the brokenness that was a reality even before Summer could put two words into a sentence.

Deep within Summer's being, in that place where she needed to feel the security of unconditional love and the delightful validation of her being, was a black hole of abandonment and loneliness. Meant to feel the nurture of tender love, instead Summer experienced disconnection from God and from her parents. They were there for her physically, but the emotional investment so critical to trust and confidence was missing. That reality set her on a course of fear, trying desperately to grab hold of what she needed in order to feel significant and safe. What she embraced, unfortunately, could never touch that core desire and empowered the darkness all the more.

In the earliest days of life, Summer had been set up to believe that the fulfillment of the basic longings of her life depended on the acceptance of others, the safety of her environment, the absence of risk and potential harm, and a flawless performance in life. So she desperately gave her all to pursuing and managing these goals to fill the emptiness deep within her soul. All the while she was aware subconsciously that the achievement of these goals was based on a fragile foundation and could collapse at any minute! As a result she was forever afraid.

Abandonment and Loneliness

Having moved forward on my own journey into that dark place and having listened to countless fellow pilgrims, I am convinced that these two realities, abandonment and loneliness, are at the center of the battle with irrational fear.

You were created to be in union with God, where you could feel the full impact of His delight and fulfilling love. Connected in that intimate embrace, you would be confident in His provision and commitment to your well-being. You would experience a sweet peace deep within, assuring you that no matter what comes your way, there are beneath you the strong arms of the heavenly Father, supporting you and carrying you through.

In God's original plan, parents would, by their love and behavior, reinforce the wonder of your identity and the security of their commitment to you. But in a fallen world, and in even the best of homes, that reality is imperfect at best, and in some cases totally absent. The result of this brokenness is a dark feeling of abandonment and loneliness that you try to manage for the rest of your life. It births great fear!

Becoming a Christian does not automatically address this issue. Many people are brought to salvation with a message of deliverance from sin and hell while missing the critical teaching of intimacy with the Father and the truth of His delight in them. The core longings of life can be lastingly filled only by experiencing union with Him. When that reality is absent, even among Christians, there results a continued and desperate search for security in things that will never satisfy that need. We turn to people, performance, possessions and other very transient substitutes—while only connecting with the Father in intimate embrace will ever fill that dark place. The absence of intimacy with God means the presence of loneliness and that dark, deep feeling of abandonment.

That, dear friend, is the real center of fear in your life.

I can hear my friend Joyce, who was raised in a Christian home, reacting to this suggestion, telling me that she had a good childhood and became a Christian at a very early age. How could her battle with fear find its core in the darkness of abandonment and loneliness? Her parents, after all, were loving, kind and supportive and God was always at the center of their home.

I understand this reaction but stand by my conclusion. The beloved disciple, John, said, "Perfect love drives out fear" (1 John 4:18). As good as the love of parents and church may be, it is not perfect. In fact, in Joyce's case, she was raised in a denomination that was somewhat legalistic and prioritized the Great Commission of Christ above all else. Too little was said about intimacy with the Lord. Granted, they were good people. But the church did not bring Joyce into true relational connection with God. And her parents were just as susceptible to conditional love as anyone else. Even the best of parents lapse into expressions of love that are manipulative or conditional or inconsistent. When they do, it reinforces in a small child the dark reality that he or she is alone in a very scary place called life. When parents' love is abusive, the darkness within is even more devastating.

Core abandonment can be touched permanently only by God's healing power. In the following chapter I will share the steps necessary to that all-important work.

Questions for Reflection and Review

1. What is the critical difference between normal fear and that which is obsessive and irrational?

2. Think of a circumstance in which you battle irrational and obsessive fear. Answer the following questions with reference to that situation:

What does anticipatory anxiety look like for you in this case?

How would you normally seek to gain control?

What compulsive and obsessive behaviors would you engage in to calm your fears?

At what point would you choose to avoid?

Have any of these steps really helped you overcome fear?

3. In what way is true change not a quick fix? Why do you often choose the quick fix?

4. What correlation can you see between Summer's deep wounds and her battle with fear? Are you able to discern any similar relationship in your own struggle?

5. What, according to this chapter, is the deepest need in your life?

Piercing the Darkness

The battle to overcome debilitating and irrational fear begins by moving into the dark place where fear gains its power. I have identified five steps to this process that, when empowered by the Holy Spirit's presence and direction, bring light and life to what was once a place of pain. Before we discuss these steps, however, let me bring out three points that are impossible to overemphasize.

First, *be sure you keep moving ahead in your journey with the Lord.* Take each step prayerfully under His guidance and direction. Don't try to force memories or make something happen. Trust the Holy Spirit to bring to your mind all that needs resolving and to reveal the truths essential to your well-being. Submit to His work and, I assure you, things will soon begin to move along for you.

Second, *remember that this is a process, not a quick fix.* Believing that you can do in a day all that I am about to suggest is ill-advised and will simply not go deeply enough. Be willing to move at the Lord's pace, trusting that patience and perseverance will reap a good harvest. You are on a pilgrimage, so pace yourself to make it to the end. Don't rush things! God is working even when you cannot see or feel the results of what He is doing in your life.

And third, *walk through these steps, if at all possible, with the support of a very few caring friends, a spiritual director or a gifted counselor.* Their help will enable you to remain centered and, most important, keep you from either moving through too quickly or else bogging down at one step and not moving on in the process. Risk vulnerability with that safe person or persons, share what you are doing and ask them to support you along the way. They cannot do your work, but their love will serve you well as you walk into the dark emptiness to meet God.

Now, the five steps.

Step 1: Embrace the Darkness

The phrase *embrace the darkness* can be intimidating! You may experience fear at the very thought of moving into the place deep within where abandonment and loneliness make their home. But friend, the only way to let that place in your life be taken over as an interior castle of the Lord's abiding is to go there in His strength and make your claim.

I realize this may sound abstract and even a bit mystical, so let's put some practical understanding to what I am suggesting. You must get in touch with your own deep loneliness and abandonment. They lie far beneath all the distractions and coping mechanisms you have embraced over the years, and they will probably be difficult for you to touch on your own. That is why you must seek the Holy Spirit's help. Ask Him to reveal the deep emptiness and all the ways you try to fill it with temporary and unsatisfying substitutes instead of God's intimate presence.

Barry is one of the friendliest and most gentle men I know. He loves kids and has spent years serving the Lord in children's ministry. He came to me wanting help combating fear. Certain areas in his life—not all that different from my own and most likely similar to yours—were wearing him out and he wanted to be free.

As we began our work, Barry shared all the Scriptures and techniques he was employing in an effort to overcome his struggle. I began to ask him questions about his early childhood and his relationship with his parents. At first he objected, unsure as to the connection between his current struggles and his early childhood experiences with his parents. He kept telling me that he believed the issue was demonic and he wanted deliverance.

There may, in fact, have been a demonic element, but my concern was to get to the ground that gave evil room to work. So I told Barry to go home and ask the Holy Spirit to show him any memories or feelings he had as a child that centered on loneliness, feeling unloved, unwanted or abandoned.

By the next week Barry arrived ready to work. He told me a variety of stories, including about his parents' divorce, and the many times he had looked to the stands in Little League and never seen his dad there cheering for him. Each of the numerous accounts had a common element: the feeling of disconnectedness.

The sense of emptiness and disconnection from parents is, as I have said, very painful for a child, making him or her feel isolated and alone. It is built on the already-existing emptiness deep within resulting from the Fall, which brought separation from God. It is a scary feeling, and a child begins to grab hold of anything to fill that void, whether performance to gain approval, people-pleasing, control or any one of countless substitutes. Such grasping is not conscious; in fact, it is often

59

difficult for adults to remember it. This is most likely because we build protective defenses early on in life to put those feelings far away from us, because they hurt so much and are very frightening.

So seek the Holy Spirit's direction in this process. Don't take my word that this is the root. Go to Him and ask. If you are battling fear, I feel confident that He will identify the feelings and events that gave birth to your struggle. When something comes to mind, perhaps as you are driving or shopping or washing dishes, write it down. That list will be important as you move to the next step in the process.

Step 2: Grieve Your Losses

Many people suffered painful events in the past that they have never properly grieved or resolved. They might not even recognize that they have been wounded, but the hurt is there just the same. What results is ongoing emotional upheaval that is often addressed in counterproductive ways.

Let's go back to the story of Barry. When he came back to me the second week with a list of several events and general feelings from his earliest memories, all linked to abandonment and loneliness, he assured me that these were far in the past and did not really affect him as an adult. I was sure he was wrong. Most of Barry's fears, plus the unhealthy ways he responded to life, were rooted, I felt, in these early events and impressions. For him to get in touch with them by the Spirit's guidance would be critical to freedom. So we prayed together, and as I asked some leading questions, Barry began to rehearse the relevant memories of past hurt. He was amazed to find surfacing a great deal of pain, pent-up emotion and destructive lies that he still believed.

There are three important questions you must ask relative to the memories and events of past hurt. First, *"How did I feel as a result of that event?"*

I asked this of Barry when he told me of his parents' divorce, which had occurred when he was five years old. At first he said, "I don't know—sad, I guess." But as I kept asking leading questions under the Spirit's direction, it was not long before Barry was crying, telling me that he had felt alone and terrified and that he wondered what he could do to keep his mom and dad from divorcing. All these feelings had been simmering since he was five, unresolved and unaddressed. These feelings had led him to the distorted conclusion that if he had been a better boy, his folks would have stayed together. Barry needed to feel and grieve this past hurt and, in God's presence, release it from his life.

A second question I ask is, *"What did I believe about myself as a result of this painful event?"* When we experience hurt associated with abandonment and loneliness, as little children we interpret it as saying something about us. This is so because significant others have become the primary source of speaking into us about our identity and worth. Before the Fall, as I have pointed out, God intended us to be secure in our identities because of our union with Him and our assurance of His delight and care. But with separation, children are affected in their identities by the earliest events and messages sent by significant others. If these messages are negative, unworthiness and abandonment are imprinted in the children's lives.

When asked this second question, Barry began to weep. He was feeling the rejection stored up from years of unresolved pain and distorted thinking. Words like *unworthy, unwanted, bad boy* and *lost* poured out, along with a great deal of emotion.

You, too, will find that your beliefs about yourself are shaped by painful feelings and events. As a child you probably found defense mechanisms that protected you. But when you become an adult, these coping strategies break down and fear grabs hold and destroys.

A third and final question is, *"How did this event affect the way I approach life?"* The goal of this question is to get you to consider how the event and message influenced your day-to-day responses to life. Such deep woundings affect the way you respond to others and especially the way you feel about yourself. For Barry they led not only to fear, but to people-pleasing, avoidance behaviors and self-contempt.

These three questions can be used, under the Spirit's empowerment, to put you in touch with that dark and painful core of your being where fear gains its strength. Asking these questions will help you grieve the past by getting you in touch with hidden pain and help you identify the consequences these events had on you. This will open the way for you to purge the dark emotion deep within and make room for the transaction with your heavenly Father that will set you free to receive His grace and peace.

Step 3: Receive an Infusion of Truth

As the darkness and distortions of abandonment and loneliness begin to drain, you need a loading dose of truth. The Scriptures to dwell on and claim at this point are related to God's love for you and the wonderful identity He has placed within you through Christ Jesus. These two categories of truth are essential to your well-being and freedom from irrational fear.

Let's go back to Barry again—a man who had carried feelings of abandonment and unworthiness his entire life. Yes, it was true that his parents did, in many ways, open the way for him to feel rejected and defective. But those feelings were not ultimate reality in Barry's life. He was chosen by God before the foundation of the earth and endowed with the very nature of Christ. Barry was an adopted child of the most high and holy God, dearly loved and an heir of Kingdom riches! Barry was in desperate need of these truths, and I encouraged him to feed on, meditate on, declare and share them until they became firm in his mind.

You probably acknowledge these truths about Barry. Are you convinced of them about yourself? You, like him, have been given countless messages, through word and deed, about unworthiness, unacceptability, abandonment and rejection. But know this: Those messages are lies born in hell, meant to keep you in the bondage of fear and self-hatred. Jesus Christ has made you a new creation through His blood, and that identity is yours as a gift of grace. Far from being abandoned and alone, you are folded into the family of God and endowed with unbelievable riches in character and ability. Frankly, God is nuts about you! He longs to meet you in that dark place and tell you about His love, devotion and everlasting commitment.

Take a season and soak in the following truths:

God is with you. "Even though I walk through the valley of the shadow of death, I will fear no evil, for you are with me; your rod and your staff, they comfort me" (Psalm 23:4).

God delights in you. "The LORD your God is with you, he is mighty to save. He will take great delight in you, he will quiet you with his love, he will rejoice over you with singing" (Zephaniah 3:17).

You have eternal life. "The wages of sin is death, but the gift of God is eternal life in Christ Jesus our Lord" (Romans 6:23).

You are not condemned. "There is now no condemnation for those who are in Christ Jesus" (Romans 8:1).

God will not separate you from His love. "I am convinced that neither death nor life, neither angels nor demons, neither the present nor the future, nor any powers, neither height nor depth, nor anything else in all creation, will be able to separate us from the love of God that is in Christ Jesus our Lord" (Romans 8:38–39).

God has made you part of Christ's body. "You are the body of Christ, and each one of you is a part of it" (1 Corinthians 12:27).

You are a new creation. "If anyone is in Christ, he is a new creation; the old has gone, the new has come!" (2 Corinthians 5:17).

You are forgiven. "In him we have redemption through his blood, the forgiveness of sins, in accordance with the riches of God's grace" (Ephesians 1:7).

God has sealed you as His. "Having believed, you were marked in him with a seal, the promised Holy Spirit" (Ephesians 1:13).

You are alive in Christ. "Because of his great love for us, God, who is rich in mercy, made us alive with Christ even when we were dead in transgressions—it is by grace you have been saved" (Ephesians 2:4–5).

You are God's workmanship. "We are God's workmanship, created in Christ Jesus to do good works, which God prepared in advance for us to do" (Ephesians 2:10).

God loves you. "I pray that out of his glorious riches he may strengthen you with power through his Spirit in your inner being, so that Christ may dwell in your hearts through faith. And I pray that you, being rooted and established in love, may have power, together with all the saints, to grasp how wide and long and high and deep is the love of Christ, and to know this love that surpasses knowledge—that you may be filled to the measure of all the fullness of God" (Ephesians 3:16–19).

You are complete. "You have been given fullness in Christ, who is the head over every power and authority" (Colossians 2:10).

God has given you access to Him. "Therefore, brothers, since we have confidence to enter the Most Holy Place by the blood of Jesus . . ." (Hebrews 10:19).

You are holy. ". . . Let us draw near to God with a sincere heart in full assurance of faith, having our hearts sprinkled to cleanse us from a guilty conscience and having our bodies washed with pure water" (Hebrews 10:22).

God wants to lavish love on you. "How great is the love the Father has lavished on us, that we should be called children of God!" (1 John 3:1).

These are but a sampling of truths that will minister to the dark core of your struggle. Ask the Holy Spirit to reveal these wonderful realities to you deep within your own spirit. Dwell with these texts, soaking in them for long seasons. Rejoice before the Lord as you do, allowing them supernaturally to bring light to the darkness and pain where fear finds its power.

Do this and you will begin to find new confidence and strength. You will come to know that you are not alone. Though others forsake you, your Father in heaven is ever present and longing to embrace you in intimate union and delight.

Step 4: Pursue Intimacy with God

For the past six years the Lord has been speaking one message repeatedly into my heart: *Pursue intimacy with Me above all else!*

For twenty years I gave all I had for Christian service. I believed mission was more important than anything else. But through the dark night of my own breakdown, I learned that I was desperately wrong.

Make no mistake—the Lord does desire our service. But His first concern is for our hearts' devotion. He wants us to spend time at His feet in sweet embrace, as Mary did (see Luke 10:38–42). Too many of us have become distracted Marthas, busy making preparations for a dinner the Lord never really asked for. Jesus warned the Church that service not issuing out of intimate knowledge of Him can be disastrous (see Matthew 7:21–23). The evidence of this imbalance is epidemic burnout among Christians and great battles with the emptiness that leads to fear.

Just the other day I had the opportunity to talk with a friend who leads a national ministry for broken people. He told me he was fighting off fatigue and fear. When I asked about his pursuit of intimacy with God, he admitted he was just not there. Little wonder fear raises its ugly head! Disconnection from God's embrace and the absence of communion with Him leads eventually to emptiness and loneliness. Fill that hole with activities and people all you want—they will never satisfy. Only union with God brings fullness and freedom.

The journey into darkness must involve a radical shift of your life, as you give far more time and attention than ever before to intimacy with God.

There are some specific tracks for that emphasis in your life. A book I have written entitled *In Pursuit of God's Embrace* focuses exclusively on this theme. It is enough here to say that you must accept this pursuit as foundational to your freedom and embrace the disciplines that help make that desire a reality.

Simply stated, consider the following activities:

Ask the Lord to birth that passion within you.
Trust that He will answer your prayer.
Be sensitive to the ways He will draw you to Himself.
Set aside time for that pursuit.

Find a special place for solitude and devotion.

Look for a person who will share your journey toward Him.

Find a spiritual director who will help you recognize God in your life.

Learn new disciplines like silence, solitude, meditation, contemplation and centering prayer.

Read literature that will help you in this pursuit. (See the Selected Bibliography on pp. 175–76.)

This pursuit is the most critical part of your journey from fear to freedom. Reconnecting with God is the central step in chasing out the darkness where fear dwells. Communion with Him is the only lasting way to address the abandonment and loneliness that give birth to your struggle. Time in His embrace brings the peace and security you need to face life and its risks. It is also the only permanent prescription for overcoming the feelings of rejection, punishment and ridicule that spring from your battle with fear.

Seek the Father above all else in your life.

Step 5: Connect with a Caring Community

The journey to freedom and intimacy with God is not one you should take by yourself. Although it is critical that you spend time alone before the Lord, it is equally important that you connect with a few people in deep friendship and support. You are made to experience such community where love and care are expressed in healthy ways. You are designed by God to be in relationship with other believers, gathering regularly to share life and to experience God's loving presence. I mean by this a level of relationship that goes beyond the normal Sunday morning experience. Gathering with other Christians to worship, hear God's Word preached and partake of His table is a vital part of the life of faith. But a deeper and more intimate connection is necessary if you want to experience the transforming power of love.

Moving successfully through the darkness of abandonment and loneliness requires a connection with a few other believers, all committed to activities like:

Speaking God's delight into one another

Expressing love and tenderness to one another

Assuring one another of God's faithful presence and care

Speaking words of encouragement to one another

Expressing grace, not judgment, to one another

Being patient with one another's brokenness

Calling one another to new life and health through Christ

Helping one another resist dysfunctional and sinful ways of coping

Providing a safe environment for one another to change

Pursuing God's embrace with one another

Celebrating the goodness of God with one another

Connecting with one another to grow and mature in Christ

Joining with one another to serve the broken and lost

I am convinced that the Lord means Christians to form small communities where we can relate to one another in these ways. Such relationships help you connect more with God in the depth of your soul, learning to trust and depend on His passionate love for you. A community like this also serves to reinforce within you the wonder and delight of who you are in Christ. Such friends repeatedly affirm the marvelous identity that is now yours because of the transforming work of the Lord. They help you resist the old lies of rejection and unworthiness that have plagued your life. They celebrate the gift of your life and call you to step beyond the patterns of brokenness and sin into freedom.

Larry Crabb has written an important book about community entitled *Connecting: A Radical New Vision* (Word, 1997). In this work Crabb calls Christians to gather in small groups of a few people and learn to love and support one another as the Lord intended. Crabb writes:

> I have come to believe that the root of all our personal and emotional problems is a lack of togetherness, a failure to connect that keeps us from receiving life and prevents the life in us from spilling over others.
>
> p. 32

He goes on to say that the majority of Christians are disconnected, and as a result struggle unsuccessfully to overcome the emotional, spiritual and psychological problems that plague them. Crabb defines disconnection as

> a condition of existence where the deepest part of who we are is vibrantly attached to no one, where we are profoundly unknown and therefore experience neither the thrill of being believed in nor the joy of loving or being loved.
>
> p. 44

Crabb is describing the very issue we are discussing in this chapter. Disconnection brings deep emptiness and isolation that give birth to fear and dysfunctional behaviors to control the world around us. To overcome fear, we must take serious steps to address that dark and scary place, including connecting with people who hunger for the level of relationship the Lord intended for His children.

Prayerfully seek out those fellow travelers and join them on the journey to intimacy and peace. Possibly you already have such friendships. If so, develop them to an even deeper level. If you are not presently enjoying fellowship such as I am describing, seek the Lord's help in identifying those people. Possibly you will need to begin such a group yourself. However it happens, get connected with other Christians, for that experience of love is a vital part of your journey to peace.

Commit to the Process

I am thoroughly convinced that the five steps we have discussed in this chapter are essential for overcoming your battle with fear. They address the deep place where fear gains its debilitating power. They are not, as I have said, a quick fix. The journey takes time and sensitivity to the work of the Lord along the way. You may even find that God will lead you into a season in the desert to accomplish this work—a place where you cannot be distracted by all the noise and defenses that separate you from your deepest hurts and wounds. I will say more about that season in the next chapter.

But if you commit to the process, you will soon find something far more exciting than simply beating irrational fear. You will discover a level of fellowship with your heavenly Father that transforms your life. You will learn to rest in His embrace and listen with joy to the whispers of His love and delight. You will find that, far from being unworthy, rejected, abandoned and alone, you are endowed with the very wonder of Christ's nature—a gifted child of the Most High, full of potential and possibility. While the battle you face is deeper than simply fear, the healing you receive is far greater than you could ever ask or think.

Questions for Reflection and Review

1. Why is it important that you allow the Lord to guide the process of identifying deep wounds?

2. What help could a spiritual director or counselor bring to this process?

3. What did I mean by embracing the darkness within you?

4. Why is it important that you grieve your losses?

5. How do the three questions listed in that section help you grieve?

6. Read each of the Scriptures listed under "Step 3: Receive an Infusion of Truth." What do these tell you about who you really are and what is truly yours?

7. Why is pursuing intimacy with God so important?

8. What steps are you willing to take in that pursuit?

9. Why is connecting with a caring community so vital? Who are these people for you?

10. Are you willing to find such a place for your own growth and well-being?

Say Yes to **6**the Desert

How do you respond to pain? For years I had only one way of dealing with discomfort, whether physical, relational, emotional or even spiritual. I would kill it with some effective anesthetic. If the pain was physical, I would take a pill. If it was relational, I would either cling to or distance myself from people. If the pain was emotional, I would find something that made me feel better, like going to a good movie or buying something new. And if spiritual, I would try to serve more aggressively to keep God happy with me. The last thing I ever did was listen to what the pain was trying to tell me—that something was wrong and needed attention. As a result I never addressed what was causing the pain in the first place. I simply eliminated the symptoms and plunged on.

This was true especially when it came to the core abandonment and loneliness I felt deep inside. Very early on I had touched that pain and it was devastating—so much so that I never wanted to feel that way again. If I got even close, I would grab for the painkillers and pop all I could to numb those dark, devastating feelings.

I had several painkillers of choice and learned to take the one appropriate to the situation. I could stay away from the pain of abandonment and loneliness through performance, building codependent relationships with certain people and distancing myself from others. I could also distract myself through a variety of activities like sports, reading, work, movies, a good meal or sex. Whenever the circumstance of my life situation brought me close to that deep, dark place, I would escape by one (and sometimes more) of my painkillers.

In his book *Reaching Out* (Doubleday, 1986), Henri Nouwen wrote about this tendency to mask the pain of our own loneliness:

> Too often we will do everything possible to avoid the confrontation with the experience of being alone, and sometimes are able to create the most ingenious devices to prevent ourselves from being reminded of this condition. Our culture has become most sophisticated in the avoidance of pain, not only our physical pain, but our emotional pain as well. We not only bury our dead as though they are still alive, but we also bury our pains as if they were not really there. We have become so used to this state of anesthesia, that we panic when there is nothing or nobody left to distract us. When we have no project to finish, no friend to visit, no book to read, no television to watch or no record to play, and when we are left all alone by ourselves, we are brought so close to the revelation of our basic human aloneness and are so afraid of experiencing an all pervasive sense of loneliness that we will do anything to get busy again and continue the game which makes us believe that everything is fine after all.

p. 27

Did this method of dealing with abandonment and lone-liness work for me? Well, in a way it did, temporarily. I was able to stay away from those horrible feelings. But my coping mechanisms, like any addiction, were not addressing the core need in my life. While I did not feel the pain, the darkness was there just the same. It was even getting stronger, and my painkillers of choice were becoming less effective. Also, many of these dysfunctional behaviors were creating their own problems in my life. Far from helping, they offered only short-term peace on the way to long-term pain. And since the dark place within was still there and growing darker, fear was becoming an increasing problem in my life.

True freedom for me, including learning to overcome fear, would come only as I got in touch with the feelings of lone-liness that lay deep inside. I had to embrace the darkness before light ever came to that frightening place. In order for this to happen, the layers of defense I had constructed through my various painkillers had to be exposed for what they truly were—enemies to health and wholeness.

The question, of course, is, "How did this happen?" The answer, simply put: God began to move me into the desert.

Into the Desert

If you have been a Christian for even a brief time, you are most likely aware that the Bible contains more than a few stories set in the desert. Whenever God wants to do a deep work in someone's life, He often leads him or her into the wilderness. In addition to the people of Israel during the exodus, Moses spent time there, as did Elisha, John the Baptist, Paul and John the apostle, to name a few. They all met God in the desert and as a result were forever transformed.

What is it about the desert that seems to make it a necessary part of the journey toward freedom?

There are two important realities present in all these wilderness stories. First, when you are in the desert, the resources to which you usually turn for comfort and support are not readily at hand. Take the children of Israel. The desert frightened them so much that they wanted to return to the bondage of Egypt. The wilderness was a scary place where water was scarce, food was hard to come by, enemies were big and strong and the going was difficult. The Israelites were on their way to freedom, but the absence of leeks, onions, melons and roofs over their heads put them into a panic. In touch with a deep sense of abandonment and loneliness, they felt exposed to great danger. They wanted to turn back, even to bondage, since it would reduce their level of fear and pain. The desert had exposed their deep brokenness and disconnectedness from God.

The second reality of the desert experience, and why it seems a necessary part of the journey toward freedom, is that God is directing it. He took the Israelites there in order to strip away the layers of their own defense against dark abandonment. He wanted to eliminate the false comfort they had enjoyed in Egypt and introduce them to a new level of relationship with Himself. He wanted them to trust Him to fulfill all their core needs, not leeks and onions and false gods. To do that He had to take them to a place where they could not easily turn back to their old ways or have access to old comforts. And during this time God was wonderfully near and attentive to their cries. They needed simply to turn to Him in their fear and pain, and He was ready to delightfully provide.

Unfortunately, most of the Israelites refused to trust the process and continually panicked, grumbled and doubted God's love. The desert made them uncomfortable and they wanted out of there. They desired to go back and even shaped a false god to lead the way. God, on the other hand, wanted them to experience freedom by moving forward with Him. As a result of their lack of trust, they had to stay in the desert far longer than the Lord had originally intended. Refusing to surrender to the process brought years and years of continued struggle. Had the Israelites turned to God in the midst of their pain, they would have realized His incredible love and the reality of His constant care and provision. They would have entered the Promised Land in a matter of months, rather than the forty years it actually took, enjoying both freedom and intimacy with their heavenly Father.

If you want to beat your struggle with fear, let God have access to the dark place where fear gets its power. If you are like most of us, that place is well defended by a variety of sophisticated coping mechanisms, including your own cache of painkillers. If the Father is to get to the core, those behaviors must be confronted and disarmed to give Him room to work. The process will certainly involve a season with Him in the desert. With your painkillers out of easy reach, you will feel the pain of abandonment and loneliness, but you will also have a chance to embrace God in your life as never before.

Freedom will be yours not by turning back to your old ways but by moving into the pain and heartache amplified by the desert experience. Let the discomfort drive you to God and let Him embrace you in that place. When you do, you will find the source of life and nourishment that will transform that dark, scary place into the garden of His delight.

The Desert of God's Choosing

In the third and fourth centuries many Christians began to leave society and escape to the deserts of Egypt, Palestine, Arabia and Persia. Some went into extreme solitude, living the life of hermits. Others formed small communities for mutual accountability and support. This movement began as a reaction to what many believed to be the secularization of Christianity. It seemed that the life of faith was being compromised and, more tragically, that the intimate presence of God was being lost to the Church. So it was that many opted for the desert in hopes of meeting God there and maintaining the spiritual and mystical elements of the faith.

I do not mention this in order to discuss either the merits or the pitfalls of this movement. I bring it up only to reinforce the impact that desert times can have on your search for freedom. The desert fathers, as they came to be known, would warn novices that they would not first meet God in the desert. Instead they would be confronted by their own true selves, long hidden by the distractions of the lives they had led in society. That confrontation would be painful because it would put them in touch with their own brokenness. But only then would they meet God in the way they longed for. Those who faced the pain and moved through it would be changed. Many, however, would grow fearful and leave before reaching that point.

The Lord in His grace has brought me into the desert several times in recent years, and on each occasion designed to bring me deeper into the place of my own pain. There, in the wilderness of His design, He has called me to release all dysfunction and distractions in order to find Him as the lasting, fulfilling source of life. Such times are not easy, nor were they meant to be. But they have been vital to my growth and freedom.

Most recently He has gone with me into what could be the most painful season of all, and through that difficult place shown me more of my broken, true self. More important, He opened my heart to His delight and unconditional love.

During this season the Lord placed me far from the people I usually turn to for support. While there is good reason to be linked with other believers for encouragement and help, He wanted me to see that I had placed some of those people in a place where only He belonged. I had looked to them to fill the loneliness of my life—an unfair expectation on them and an unhealthy approach to meeting a core need in my own life. God moved me physically to a spot where I could not turn to others to ease my pain. As a result the pain initially caused me almost to come unglued.

Central to this season was being separated from my two oldest children, Aaron and Cara. They are both adults and lived near us in Northern California. They are the most wonderful people, and I have always loved being around them. In fact, I have always felt better, no matter what the struggle, when they and their younger sister, Emily, have been near. But in 1997 the Lord led Cheryl, Emily and me to leave California and make our way to Ohio. Along the way we stopped in Colorado to receive much-needed spiritual direction and counseling.

Colorado is a beautiful state; for years I had wanted to live there. I love the mountains, and fishing is one of my favorite pastimes. So I arrived there full of excitement, wondering what good thing the Lord wanted to do in my life. It was not long, however, before I felt an intense loneliness. My closest friends were in California—and, more important, Aaron and Cara.

As the days turned to weeks, the pain of that separation became excruciating. I missed them and felt despair about their decision not to accompany us. For some time I struggled, and finally began to seek the Lord about all this upheaval. I soon learned that the time apart from them was divinely ordered, placing me at a distance where they could not kill my pain.

One morning I found myself in tears as I thought of them, and there met the Lord in a deep and revealing way. I wrote of it in my journal that day and am including the entry here. Though long, it may open a window to your own struggle.

What I am about to address goes far, far deeper than the presenting issue. I know that beneath the pain of the presenting matter is a work of the Lord that must be done in my life. I also know that the circumstance of all the changes going on, particularly the separation I feel from those I love so, is of Him and good. But I dare not pretend that there is not pain, for to do so would keep me from finding the Lord there and growing as He would so desire.

Last night I wrestled in bed, sleeping fitfully. At one point I had a dream that Aaron and Cara had come to visit. I have no idea where the place was, but knew that they had come to spend some time. How wonderful and good it was to be with them, to touch them, to love them. I remember feelings of deep joy and contentment at their presence, so near and sweet. I looked at Aaron's hands, remembering his childhood with delight. I could smell him in the dream, feel his whiskers against my face and hear him laugh. I stared at Cara's smile, felt her arms around me and felt so satisfied to hear her call out, "Daddy." But they came to me and announced that they were now leaving to return to California, a week earlier than expected. I began to weep and hold them so close. And I distinctly remember saying to them, "I need you in my life to feel whole."

I awakened this morning with deep pain, a longing for them. I know in part this is related to their telling me this week that they would not be coming to Ashland for an extended stay this summer. Admittedly this saddened me. But the issue here is far deeper and goes well beyond Aaron and Cara. It goes to my core sense of abandonment and loneliness that has plagued me for ever so long. It is most certainly related to the fears the Lord is now addressing.

With all the changes these days have brought, the core loneliness of my life has come to the surface, and I see it as never before, and see how I managed it in ways that left me dependent and wanting. I see that I have long felt alone, abandoned and rejected—all from core childhood wounds and reinforced by other relationships. The pain of this has been too much for me, and so throughout my life I have killed the pain with countless distractions and anesthetizing activities. I have worked, and played, and eaten, and achieved, and held onto my children, my wife and my friends, so as to keep the deep feelings put away, put far away.

But in this season all these have been, or are being, stripped away, exposing within the wound from which all other wounds receive their power and pain. The issue here is not separation from others. The core issue is a separation deep within myself, a feeling of rejection that has birthed loneliness and resulted in pain. But today I not only see how I have hidden and sought to satisfy this pain in really bad ways; I also hear Him calling to me from the very darkness I have sought to avoid. To love others, desire their presence, miss them when apart is good and even healthy. But in my dream I said, "I need you in my life to feel whole." Therein lies the festering wound. There is the problem.

I have tried to fill a void with people and things that can be filled only with the Lord. I have clung too tightly and given a power to people they were never meant to have, all to kill that dark and desperate feeling that I am alone. There have been sweet moments in relationship, for sure—some life-changing. But there have also been unhealthy dependencies and, as with this summer, deep fears of being alone, even panic when I could find no one there for me. But the Lord has brought me to a place of facing what was not good in this issue, and even placed in my life caring friends who encouraged me to let go of the need for others, in order to be fulfilled forever in the richness of union with my God and my Lord, who loves me as none other.

And so yet again I am wooed into the pain, to find there the Healer who longs to touch the core wound that has crippled me for so long. As the painkillers are rendered ineffective or unavailable, I hurt. Tears are there, surfacing in my eyes from a place deeper than an artesian well. But it is in that place, where the sorrow starts, that He smiles and beckons me to come.

As I embrace the moment, I sense that His presence will satisfy, finally, a hunger that has gnawed at me since childhood. Fulfilled in His arms, I believe I will now go to embrace others—wife, children, friends, the broken, the lost—not out of need but out of overflowing passion and desire. I will come to others not out of my own emptiness but out of the overflow of my walk with Him that satisfies the cry of my broken heart.

I have been greatly affected by the Exodus, and was moved by the Lord's setting apart the Levites for Himself. I was stirred. Could it be that I am a Levite, my heart fully meant to be filled with Him alone, so that I will never again struggle with being alone? Such oneness will not mean there is not sorrow and sadness when separation looms. But it will be healthy pain that has a sweetness and joy to it, rather than the constant fear that abandonment is my lot, and panic is ever close.

I know there is more to consider here—far more. But once again the Lord has used the pain of a current circumstance to lead me to the deeper place where He longs to meet me and set me free. Will I still long to see and hold my children and friends? I am sure I will. And there will be tears. But I sense that there will also be serendipitous delight even then. The Lord will be there—is there, even now as I write—to hold me close and assure me that He loves me. He longs to see and hold me, to feel my whiskers against His face, to look at my hands and delight in me forever. I can hardly see to write, for I am crying from a place far deeper than words can express. Someone does love me and long for me. Someone wants to share my pain, hear my concerns, laugh and look at me. There is emotion greater than I felt about Aaron and Cara. God thinks of me like that. He longs to embrace me and loves being with me. I am a sobbing mess right now and I can write no more. He is here right now. I turn into His arms.

That morning brought a profound encounter with God I will never forget. The separation that God designed brought about a union I would never have known otherwise. I allowed Him to enter the darkness of my own loneliness, all because He placed me far from those I loved and depended on most. Leaning on others to fill that need was wrong. God showed me that and, more important, moved me into the desert where their touch was out of reach and His presence closer than hands and feet.

Instructions for the Desert

You, too, must be willing to be led into the desert of God's choosing. Your distractions and escape mechanisms only serve to isolate you from God and others. As a result fear will be your constant companion. I have no idea what that season will look like for you. But if you cry out humbly and honestly for God's help, He will lead you there.

It will not be a place of punishment. God will draw you close and embrace you in love. His word in Hosea 2:14 assures you of His good intention. Speaking of His love for Israel, God declares, "I am now going to allure her; I will lead her into the desert and speak tenderly to her." What He did for the Israelites, He will do for you as well.

So whatever you do, don't turn back to the false gods and leeks and onions of your old way of coping. Allow God to do His work. He longs to go into the dark place where fear is born and turn it into a garden of His delights. You will experience some pain, possibly even excruciating. Don't run from it or rush to numb yourself senseless.

Walk into it, fear and all. There you will find your Father waiting to love you beyond your wildest dreams.

The desert broke many Israelites because they did not respond to it properly. In my own search for help, therefore, I turned to Psalm 106 and there found several practical admonitions on how to move forward in this season. I included these in a book I have already mentioned, entitled *In Pursuit of God's Embrace,* but believe it important to share them here. During desert times God's Word instructs you to:

Believe His promises (verse 12)

Sing His praise (verse 12)

Remember what He has done for you in the past (verse 13)

Wait for His counsel (verse 13)

Do not give in to sinful desires (verse 14)

Do not envy others (verse 16)

Do not turn to familiar idols (verse 19)

Do not despise the place where God has put you (verse 24)

Believe His promise (verse 24)

Do not grumble (verse 25)

Obey the Lord (verse 25)

Do not strike out in anger (verse 33)

Cry out to God in humility (verse 44)

Praise the Lord (verse 48)

These admonitions will serve you well as you move through the wilderness with the Lord. Soak in the truths they offer, and you will find that His strength and presence will carry you through to freedom.

From here we will look at several destructive false premises that engender fearful responses in your life. They must be rooted out if you are to progress on the pathway to peace and freedom.

Questions for Reflection and Review

1. What are the distractions and painkillers you use to keep the pain at bay?

2. Why is it necessary that they be set aside in your pursuit of wholeness?

3. Why did the Lord take His people into the desert?

4. How did they react to this season and what was the result?

5. Have you ever been through a desert season? Why did God take you there? What did you learn?

6. What are the false gods and leeks that enticed you?

7. How should you respond to such times? Refer to Psalm 106.

Recognizing the Distortions That Empower Fear

7

W hat have you learned so far about conquering fear? First, as we discussed in the first three chapters, you must be open and vulnerable before the Lord regarding your struggle. Masking your battle only intensifies it. In chapter 4 we saw that fear is really a symptom of your deeper battle with abandonment and loneliness. Within you is a dark place of emptiness where fear gains its power. The key to wholeness is allowing God to fill that chasm, for He alone is the source of light and life. We discussed the steps to filling it in chapter 5. Finally we discussed the importance of identifying and eliminating the painkillers and distractions that keep you from feeling the core of pain deep within your life. God often accommodates this process by leading you lovingly into a season in the desert. There you face your pain and press into the Lord to discover the wonder and security of His embrace.

In this chapter we will see that moving forward in the journey involves recognizing and renouncing the false premises that keep us reacting to life from a fear base, rather than from trust in God's goodness and love. You have most likely embraced certain reactions (however improper and immature) as responses to your own woundedness. Unfortunately these induce great fear and keep you in never-ending anxiety and discomfort as you struggle to kill the ceaseless pain of abandonment. These false premises must be demolished for the lies they are, as you lay hold of the truth that will free you from obsessive and irrational fear. Only by recognizing and renouncing these reactions as lies will you move on to the peace that can be yours in the Lord.

Remember, the core wound beneath them is your own sense of abandonment and loneliness. The emptiness itself is not a lie. But your response to it as an immature and unknowing child—rather than admit its reality, then invite God (who alone can fill the core needs of your life) into that place to bring you fellowship, intimacy, strength and peace—was probably to embrace certain lies as the correct way to respond. These have led to behaviors that may numb the pain but will never heal you at the core.

What happens when you discover, as a very small child, that you are alone? It does not take long for a vulnerable child to realize that the world is a very scary place. You have genuine core longings, like desires for meaning, love, security and acceptance. The question is, How are these needs to be met?

In God's original design, parents would have served to meet your basic needs, all the while working to connect you with your heavenly Father. They would have loved you unconditionally, spoken the truth of who you are into your identity, and kept you safe and secure in a dangerous world. As you grew, they would have moved you to know God more and more and taught you to find Him as the source for your life. They would have led you to rest securely in Him. In that design you would not have grown up to react in fear to life, but would be experiencing His strength and peace.

Most parents just do not do that. Sometimes they even make the world seem *more* frightening by reacting aggressively or insensitively. Instead of being there for your safety and security, they did things that scared you and increased your feelings that the world is unsafe. They may not have been present for you, either emotionally or physically. What are you to do, then, to feel protected and cared for?

What follows is a list of false premises that, over the years, may have engendered fearful responses in you. All, or a combination of several, may be present in your life.

"It's All Up to Me"

Countless men and women determined early on in life that the only way to be safe and have their core needs met was to do it themselves. So they learned to walk through life isolated and independent, developing their own strategies for self-provision and protection. They had to, because no one was there for them. Whether through manipulation, aggression, deception, performance, people-pleasing or any one of several other behaviors, they learned as children to meet some of their basic needs themselves. In adulthood this strategy serves to get them what they want. But such dysfunctional behavior only isolates them all the more.

Just the other day I was talking with Paul Burns, one of my dearest friends, about his father. Paul told me that his dad trusts no one. Even when Paul was small, his father had no contact with his own brothers, sisters and parents.

Because he carried this approach to life into his marriage, he divorced Paul's mom long ago. Today he lives in Arizona in virtual isolation. He is wealthy and can buy almost anything he wants, but he lives every day afraid that someone will take away what he has. He has reacted to his own pain by disconnecting from people—and from God. As a result he lives a fearful and empty existence.

The answer to abandonment and loneliness is not trying to get through life meeting your own needs, suspicious of everything and everyone. That is a sure prescription for fear. No, the answer, as we have already discussed, is to connect with the Father who loves you with an everlasting love. He longs to meet you in the center of your being and be the sole resource for your deepest needs. He created you for that level of intimacy.

Going it alone is a false premise on which to build a life and it leads to painful isolation and emptiness. That darkness in turn keeps you forever battling deep, obsessive and irrational fear. I will discuss this at greater length in the following two chapters. Here it is enough to know that the "It's-all-up-to-me" premise is rooted in the Fall and never, ever brings fulfillment. Satan told Eve she did not need God, and he tries to convince you and me of the same thing. It is a lie, plain and simple.

"I'm Responsible for You/ You're Responsible for Me"

Ruth's mother died when she was a baby and her father passed away before she was five. She was then sent to her aunt and uncle and raised in their small home along with their five children. Her relatives provided physically but did not give her the love and affection of parents. Ruth spent her childhood feeling alone and abandoned. Her earliest memories are of great fear that she would spend her life with no one to care for her. Like all of us, she wanted to be loved and cherished, to feel that someone was there for her.

Ruth married as a teenager, in part to get away from home and, more importantly, to feel connected and cared for. But shortly she realized that her husband was not meeting the deep need she had felt all her life. The truth is, neither he nor anyone else could ever meet that need. Rather than turn to God to fill that deep void, however, Ruth turned her hopes to her children. She saw her two daughters and son as the answer to her prayers. Now she was not alone. These infants belonged to her, and she often remarked, "They're mine!"

Controlling and possessive, Ruth raised her children with a tight grip. She was quick to communicate her displeasure if the children did not act and behave as she desired. She would punish quickly and distance herself from them in order to modify their behavior, so they got the point that what they had done was unacceptable. Fear of rejection kept the children in line. It also set them up for serious problems as they grew into adults.

The three children were, in fact, painkillers, meant to anesthetize Ruth's deep feelings of abandonment and loneliness. What an awful and overwhelming burden to place on them! Ruth imprinted their soft hearts from infancy with the message that their purpose in life was to meet her core need. When they fulfilled this expectation, they received nurture and acceptance. When they did not, they were punished and rejected. To be in relationship with their mother, they learned, they had to die to themselves and serve her seemingly bottomless needs. But this great expectation fueled tremendous fear in their lives. How could they ever meet all those needs?

Ruth's son, Gary, carried the distorted impression into adult life not only that it was his responsibility to meet his mother's needs, but that he had to fill others' needs as well. If they were safe, it was because he was diligent enough. If they felt worthwhile, it was because he was faithful to encourage and compliment. If they were happy, it was because he was doing his job. Gary believed that to be in relationship and not to experience abandonment, he had to be vigilant in his relationships with others. But the subconscious realization that he could never adequately fulfill the demand kept him locked in fear. On the one hand, he wanted to do whatever possible to please. But on the other hand, he wanted to run from relationships and never look back.

God's Word talks a great deal about life with "one another." But nowhere does it say that you are responsible to meet the core needs in other people. Their fulfillment in life is not your responsibility! Yes, children are, for a season, dependent on their parents. But the word *dependent* has nothing to do with adult relationships. You and I are meant to depend on God alone as the source of our core longings.

We are to enjoy a healthy connection with others, as we discussed earlier. I will detail the nature of relationships in the next chapter. It is enough here to say that the "I'm-responsible-for-you/You're-responsible-for-me" premise is destructive and unfounded in God's design for abundant life. If for whatever reason you have embraced this notion, the time has come to reject it and learn a new way, God's way, based on love.

"Peace Is Based on My Being in Control"

If you are like me, control is important to you. This is particularly true when a situation has the potential to hurt you in some way. The harm might be physical or it might involve ridicule, embarrassment or punishment. Deep inside, you sense you are risking rejection, which would

open you to the core darkness of abandonment and loneliness. The very thought produces fear in you. So to avoid
that possibility, you respond by doing anything to control
the situation.

I know this false premise well. My own core woundings
of separation from God and, at times, imperfect love from
parents affected me deeply, communicating the message
that a situation out of control leads to great pain. To survive a potentially risky circumstance, I had to be in control.

When I was six or seven, my teenage sister acted in a play
at church sponsored by her youth group. Hanging around
as I did, I ended up getting an assignment. At one point the
lights were to be turned off during the performance and I
was to plug in the spotlight for the next act. On the night
of the play, while people filled the Sunday school room, I
was nervous and concentrating fully on my responsibility.
The moment came. The lights went out. And suddenly I
was faced with a major dilemma: *Where is the light socket?* I
scratched the plug all over the wall trying to do my job. The
lapse in time was growing longer; the audience could hear
my desperate efforts to plug in the light. Finally someone
turned on the main light and I quickly plugged the spot
into the wall. Everyone was laughing, and as I looked over
my shoulder, I could see by the disappointment on the
director's face that I had failed. I was humiliated.

This kind of event threatens rejection, and the pain is so
great that you will do almost anything to avoid it. What I
carried away from that experience was to be prepared,
almost to the point of perfectionism. I learned everything I
could, as I grew older, and worked harder than most to be
the one in charge. It was the only way I could survive—so
I thought. I tried to become the best at what I did and the
leader of most situations. Fear drove me to be in control.

People manifest this fear in countless ways. They ride
in cars only if they can drive. They seldom do anything

new or threatening. They take charge of relationships and tasks. They avoid risky situations like the plague! Their goal: to achieve peace by being in control.

But anyone truly awake to the reality of life knows that control is an illusion. You can reduce risk, yes, but eliminating the potential for hurt is impossible. You can be the best driver in the world and get killed by a falling rock from the roadside. You can insist that you coordinate the wedding and still have the groom show up late and foul up the ceremony. You can prepare for your speech and have a child start crying in the middle of your best point, distracting everyone. You can jog, eat the right foods and monitor your cholesterol levels only to die of a brain aneurysm.

I always prepared well for my sermons, priding myself in my ability to preach without notes. I would stand before the congregation in peace, confident that I could deliver God's Word effectively. I worked hard at developing this skill, only to lose it all during my bout with agoraphobia. Suddenly I was scared to death in front of a crowd, fearing that I would go blank and be humiliated. This fear hit me from behind; I was no longer in control! The very thought almost undid me. But by God's grace it ultimately led me to a new, more secure foundation: trust in Him.

The problem with control is believing it will bring you peace and keep you from the dark place of abandonment and loneliness. That is the wrong foundation for your well-being. There is always a degree of risk, no matter who is in control. Peace must not be based on your ability to perform perfectly, for anything can threaten to undo what you have worked so hard to control. Serenity comes when you know God's love and trust that He is for you in life, able to work all things for good on your behalf. It comes when you move into life confident in your Father's love and commitment to be there for you, no matter what comes your way.

Should we prepare well in life? Of course. That is good stewardship. But don't base your peace on that preparation, for factors are always present beyond your control. Rather, be ever confident of your Father's love, knowing that no matter what happens, He will never reject you and will always embrace you in His tender arms of unconditional love.

"I'm at Peace When No Risk Is Involved"

In many ways this false premise relates to the one we just discussed. But there is enough to distinguish it, demanding further attention here.

I grew up flying with my dad at the local airport and then spent years traveling across the states doing ministry. I loved flying. But all that came to a screeching halt on the flight to Tulsa. Why? I asked that question for years, and for the most part came up empty. But one day as I was trying to work through my fear, I saw that I had based my willingness to fly on a false premise. I had convinced myself that it was risk-free. Nothing bad would ever happen to me on a flight, I thought, so I boarded planes with confidence. On the flight before my Oklahoma trip, however, my illusion was challenged. An airliner crashed that very day. I read the details in the paper and was saddened by the loss of life. It did not register at the time that the accident had blighted my own sense of safety. But from that moment on I grew increasingly nervous, until the full-blown panic during my flight to Tulsa.

I had built my peace, you see, on a false foundation. Flying, although one of the safest means of travel, is not risk-free. Build that illusion and when it is destroyed, you will find yourself full of fear. I should have based my ultimate confidence not on airline safety records but on the Lord's presence and good purposes for me, regardless of the level of risk. I should have been concentrating on my connection with His love more than on reading countless books about the safety of air travel. My fear became uncontrollable because I had built my peace on an imperfect foundation.

God is the ultimate foundation of your peace. To experience the quiet confidence that you will always and ultimately be secure in Him, regardless of what happens, you must come to rest in His loving arms.

On television last evening I watched an interview with two survivors of the *Titanic* disaster. Their comments were revealing. One said, "We were living in an age when people were telling us that life was becoming easier and easier and safer and safer. This tragedy brought us to reality." The second survivor ended her comments with a familiar commentary: "The *Titanic* is a monument to man's arrogance. They told my mother, who was rather afraid, that even God could not sink the Titanic. And so she brought us on board."

It is wonderful that travel, for example, is increasingly safe and that the field of medicine (for another example) is making advances. But linking your peace to human achievement will eventually end in fear. There are always risks—some small, others great. Peace in life must ultimately be grounded on God's love for you and His commitment to see you through, regardless of the risk or hurt that comes your way.

"When All Else Fails, I Find Peace through Avoidance"

Bill Walters was only 33 when his doctor told him he needed open heart surgery. Bill had abused his body through drugs, alcohol and tobacco, and his actions had taken a tremendous toll on his health. Without the operation Bill was a walking time bomb, yet he refused to go through with the procedure.

96

Bill called me and invited me to his home one evening to discuss the situation. I knew Bill because he had been attending our church. He and his wife, Carol, had turned to the Lord recently and were trying to put their broken lives back together. But that night I saw fear in Bill's eyes. He was not afraid of surgery so much as he was of being put to sleep for the operation. The thought of being anesthetized had him in a panic and he refused to be moved from his decision.

There were two issues that really frightened Bill. First, he knew there was a small degree of risk in being put to sleep and he would have none of it. Second, being under an anesthetic meant that he would not be in control.

"Bill," I asked, "would you want them to do this procedure with you awake?" If he considered the ramifications, I thought, he might change his mind.

"If they can somehow do this with me awake," he replied, "fine. But they're not putting me under!"

Being anxious about such an operation is not in itself irrational. It is a natural response—one to be presented before the Lord in prayer. But Bill's attitude was not based on sound thinking. He was out of control about being out of control!

That was fifteen years ago. To this day Bill has not had the operation. He carries nitroglycerin pills with him everywhere and has had to radically reduce what he does, to the point of almost total disability. But Bill still insists he will not be put to sleep. He has chosen to find relief from his fears through avoidance, even at the price of his health.

Bill's story may seem extreme but it contains the basic elements of a very common false premise. Many people choose to find peace from what they perceive as uncomfortable and risky situations by avoiding them altogether.

In chapter 4 I told of my own avoidance behavior in response to agoraphobia. As a result I can understand what

97

was driving Bill, because I have been there. At the time I was desperate to escape frightening panic attacks, so I avoided any place where I might experience one. Soon I was avoiding malls, restaurants, driving alone and being apart from my wife, to name just a few. Did avoidance help? Absolutely not! In the long run I had to battle my way back by confronting every place from which previously I had run. Avoidance will, when used in response to obsessive and irrational fear, simply reduce your world.

You may be avoiding places, activities, situations, people who make you feel uncomfortable, and any one of a hundred other issues. For some reason you interpret these as potentially risky, so you just stay away. If you do, know that the premise you have latched onto—that avoidance brings peace—is, when it comes to obsessive and irrational fear, false. The long-term effect is not peace but ongoing bondage. As you choose avoidance to eliminate fear, it actually has the opposite effect. Fear gains power every time you turn and run.

Consider again the children of Israel during the exodus. They sent their spies to the Promised Land, heard about the size of their enemies and lost heart. Refusing to go forward, they chose to avoid confrontation because they believed they would be defeated. They were reading the situation from their own limited perspective. They had forgotten about God and the promise of His help and intervention. They were only to step forward and do the possible, and God would do the rest. Instead they turned back toward bondage.

That is precisely what you and I do each time we run because of irrational fear. We are forgetting God and not resting confidently in His promised care and love, but reacting to the circumstance out of the dark place of abandonment and fear.

Two things are necessary. First, address the core long-ing in your life by growing ever closer to the Father. Spend time in His presence, hear His whispers of love and delight, and feel the strength of His arms supporting you, no mat-ter what comes your way. Second, renounce this false premise for the lie it is. Avoidance as a method of reduc-ing irrational fear only breeds more fear. Learn to walk ahead in the security of God's good purposes in your life. He is with you, no matter what comes your way.

Say No to the Lies

Do you remember Summer? She built her entire life on *all* these false premises and was anxiously doing whatever possible to maintain her fragile peace. All the while, deep inside, she knew that at any moment the entire house of cards could come fluttering down. What was the result? She was exhausted, encased in obsessive and irrational fear and relating dysfunctionally to those around her. She wor-ried constantly that someone would be hurt because of her, or get mad and reject her or suddenly leave her all alone. That possibility brought devastating fear. So Summer spent her life trying desperately to keep that from happening. How? By investing in the lies we have been discussing. They never, ever served to truly bring her peace.

If you have embraced any or all of these false premises, the time has come for you to recognize their destructive power and renounce them for the evil lies they are. Only by saying no to them will you be able to move on to expe-rience the truth of God's ever-faithful love that brings light and life to the dark abandonment and loneliness you fear. He longs to be the source of fulfilling your core longings. He alone can satisfy the ache that has driven you to respond fearfully to life. These false premises bring momentary peace at best, all the while empowering the dark place within where fear gains its strength.

Allowing the Lord to help you reject these lies will take you farther along on your journey to freedom and peace. He is there for you right now, calling out to be your ever-present help in time of need. Respond to Him by running—not away from your pain and dark sense of loneliness, but directly into that place that has frightened you for so long. God is there, waiting to meet you and set you free.

Questions for Review and Reflection

1. What is the relationship between your fear and false premises?

2. What is the central distortion of the "It's-all-up-to-me" premise?

3. In what ways can a parent communicate to a child that the child is responsible for the parent's well-being?

4. What effect would this have on a child? What is the truth?

5. What is wrong with the "Peace-is-based-on-my-being-in-control" premise?

6. What is the illusion of a risk-free life? Where should your peace ultimately be grounded?

7. In what way does avoidance offer short-term peace yet long-term bondage?

8. Why must you renounce these false premises in your life?

9. What do I mean when I say that God longs to be your source?

Is Love Really
All You Need?

A re you old enough to remember the events that took place in the United States in the middle to late 1960s? I was a teenager at the time, soon to graduate from high school and preparing to go off to college. Because I was very impressionable, I found those difficult days important in shaping my understanding of right and wrong. It seemed at the time that the entire country was divided on critical social and political issues, creating great tension and suspicion between people. Chaos and confusion reigned in almost every major city in America. Many were protesting the injustice that the majority had propagated on the poor and minority groups.

Martin Luther King and Bobby Kennedy were seeking to work for change through nonviolent protest and legislative reform. Both were assassinated. In Southeast Asia men, women and children were dying in a war that had grown increasingly unpopular around the world. Young people across the nation were protesting, burning draft cards and demonstrating on college campuses. Often these acts of civil disobedience were peaceful and nonviolent. At times, however, as frustration and suspicion grew, violence erupted and National Guard troops were sent to control it. The tragedy of Kent State University, where four students were killed in 1970, will always remind us of those painful days.

Countless young people spoke out against the "establishment," a popularized term referring to existing structures of government, education and religion. Many had become convinced that the establishment was self-serving, deceptive and driven by greed. Some were calling for revolution, which frightened others who felt comfortable within the existing forms and expressions of social, political and religious life. Their reactions only widened the gap polarizing the American people.

I recall a great deal of anger and fear about those days. A pervasive spirit of competition drove people to do whatever necessary to get and keep what they believed essential to life. The unrest and confusion of the times played right into everyone's deepest fears. Many were afraid that what they needed most to make it in this world was being ripped off from them, and as a result they were crying foul. Some were warring with words; others had embraced far more aggressive means to get and keep what they wanted. Malcolm X, who was later assassinated, predicted a day when blacks would employ "any means necessary" to prevent injustice.

In the midst of those fearful and violent days arose a counterculture petitioning for peace. They began to place flowers in gun barrels and lift two fingers, the peace sign, as an appeal to stop the hurting and killing. During what became known as the summer of love, the Beatles suggested that they had found the solution to society's dilemma, declaring, "All you need is love."

At the time those words seemed little more than a Band-Aid offered to help people who had just stepped on land mines. The cry seemed particularly impotent and ineffectual because of the expressions of love that came in response. In most places it was little more than a license to stay in denial and spend days (or months) in drug use and free love. The words did not strike a blow for sanity and peace. Walking around saying, "I love you" just did not cut to the core of the problems that had surfaced in society.

But today, thirty years later, I realize the Beatles almost had it. They came close to the real answer to the poverty, war, suspicion, anger and fear that were (and still are) present among people groups across the globe. The only way to address the insecurity that gives birth to fear, resulting in an aggressive spirit of competition, is to be changed forever by love. Not the imperfect love of people—that will never bring about such radical transformation. It takes an encounter with perfect love. Only when men, women and children experience the immeasurable and unsearchable riches of God's love will they be at peace—secure and safe in this broken world.

Imperfect Love Gives Birth to Fear

Centuries ago the apostle John gave the world the answer it had been waiting to hear. In his first epistle he held out the key to overcoming the debilitating battle with fear. He wrote, "There is no fear in love. But perfect love drives out fear" (1 John 4:18).

These are some of the most important words of truth ever written. When you consider the heartbreak and violence that fear has engendered, you realize these words

103

can turn your life upside down! They can change the way you approach life and set you free from innumerable behaviors that are wearing you to a frazzle. This truth has the power to transform the way you relate to people, respond to risk and react to tragedy and death. These words are absolutely powerful.

Having said that, however, I need to make a confession. Almost every time I battled fear in the past, I read and reread this passage and simply could not get it. I had the hardest time understanding what it was saying! I would quote it aloud, receive it from concerned friends, write it in my journal and still come up empty. The problem was not putting together the theological principle. For some reason the truth of the passage did not sink into my life where the problem gained its power. It was extremely frustrating. I knew John was presenting me with the key to overcoming my struggle, but I could not fit that key into the lock and release the chains of my bondage to fear.

In the next chapter we will look directly at John's admonition that perfect love drives away fear. But in this chapter I want to discuss why that Scripture does not readily help most people in their battle with fear.

I am sure it was by the leading of God that I decided to sneak up on this text. I began to look at the opposite of what it was saying. If perfect love drives out fear, then imperfect love must give birth to fear.

In considering this truth, I realized that many of the expressions of love I had known as a child were imperfect, as they are for every human being since the Fall. Love was defined for me, when my heart was soft and impressionable, by the actions of the people around me. And because these people, like everyone, were broken, they imprinted on my heart definitions of love that were imperfect and incorrect. But as a child I did not know that. I accepted what I learned and experienced as true and went into life defining love in those terms.

As a result I did not have the categories to understand, as a Christian adult, what perfect love even looked like. I would simply read the passage in 1 John, define it by my own understanding of love, shaped years before, and impose that definition on the text. As a result it never hit me what the passage was saying. Only when God led me to understand and reject imperfect love could I begin to feel the impact of the truth John was declaring.

Imperfect love gives birth to fear because it is never really unconditional and constant. As a child you felt the pain of your own abandonment and loneliness and were desperate to get whatever you could to calm the agonizing discomfort. The natural place for you to turn for satisfaction was to your parents and significant others. Their words and touch and attention and care could bring you a sense of peace and safety.

It may be that many memories of their love are tender and edifying to your life. Unfortunately you also encountered expressions of love that were far from perfect. The Fall assured that. Sometimes the love you were given was inconsistent, selfish, manipulative, controlling and possessive. At times adults may have punished you and distanced themselves when you failed to please them or do what was right in their eyes. There may have been occasions when, preoccupied by their own needs, they were just not there for you. They may have even abused you physically, emotionally or sexually.

Whatever the actual events, your parents' actions defined love for you and influenced the way you now approach life. You, like your parents or significant others, have been blighted by the Fall; and being disconnected from the Source led you to love others as imperfectly as you were loved. There are within you patterns of behavior that you call love yet are selfish, inconsistent, manipulative and controlling. Why? Because the core abandonment of your life remains and frightens you deeply. It is the darkness that fuels your fear and leads you to respond to life in the anxious, competitive, aggressive way you do.

Nowhere is the product of imperfect love more identifiable than in the way you relate to others.

The Clenched Fist

There is no more telling symbol of imperfect love than the clenched fist. I see, as I look at my life, that the fist best represents the way I have related to people and responded to risk.

There are at least five representations of the clenched fist, each revealing a different characteristic of the fruit that imperfect love brings to life.

The Uptight Fist

With abandonment and loneliness at the core, and the resultant fear ever present within, you and I have closed our hands, made tight fists and reacted toward life in ways that never address our deepest needs.

Imperfect expressions of love never satisfy and leave you feeling insecure and hypersensitive in relationships. You are constantly reading people to see if they are accepting you or not. An unexplained glance or inappropriate comment or the slightest change in voice tone produces anxiety deep within your soul. You begin to think, *Is he upset? Did I do something wrong? Is she cutting me off?* The very thought produces fear because beneath that possibility lies potential rejection that is painful and frightening.

The result? Contradictory feelings of running to fix what may be wrong and running away because you are tired of playing the game.

First, fixing what may be wrong. Many of us respond to our nervous tension by trying constantly to please others. Guy was just such a person. He was always reading people to see what he could do to keep them liking him. He would find out what they wanted and get it without being asked. If his friends did something that signaled displeasure with him, Guy was right there with a saccharine façade trying to make them happy again. He would do almost anything, including change himself, if necessary, in order to keep people satisfied. As a result Guy was forever nervous around his friends, afraid they would find some reason to reject him and leave him all alone. He was unwilling to really be himself, afraid others would find him unacceptable. To Guy, being in relationship meant doing and being whatever he thought others wanted. That imperfect understanding of love kept him forever uptight.

The uptight fist approach to relationships also leads to running away, both on your part and on the parts of those you are in relationship with. Uptight people wear others out, sending messages constantly that they are anxious if things are not perfect. Continual checking—"Is everything O.K.? Are you upset with me? Have I done something wrong?"—makes the relationship more work than rest. It leaves little opportunity to relax and enjoy one another for the broken yet wonderful people you are. It grants no permission to have a problem that is not taken personally. It provides no space to grow individually, or to grow together as friends. And without space, friendships simply die.

Eventually the uptight fist approach leads you to run from a relationship. Tired of managing and giving yourself away, you finally separate yourself from others, trying to kill your pain by another inappropriate means. Imperfect love, though you may not have defined it as such, leaves you empty, disconnected and full of fear. It is

unsatisfying and leaves you to battle the dark emptiness
that grips your inner being.

The Grabbing Fist

Abandonment and loneliness are so frightening that
killing the pain is almost a life-and-death matter. You will
do just about anything to keep yourself from these feelings, and if you perceive that someone can meet your need,
you grab hold and won't let go.

I know, because I did this very thing in my relationships
with my wife and children. I did not try to control everything they did, but I had to know they were there. Without them, I thought, I would not be able to make it in life.
The idea of being separated (as I indicated in my journal
regarding my separation from Aaron and Cara) would lit-
erally undo me. I had convinced myself it was because I
loved them so deeply. I do, of course, but the truth is, my
grip on their lives was out of fear.

I will never forget a line from the movie *Jerry Maguire*.
A co-worker, commenting on the main character's pattern
of relationships, says, "Jerry's problem is that he can't stand
being alone." That was me through and through. I could
not stand the thought of not having someone there for me.
As a child I had caught or been taught the notion that my
well-being depended on having someone in my life who
would love me (by my own dysfunctional definition of
love, of course). As a result I always had a girlfriend or close
pals who were there for me.

I transferred this dependency to Cheryl and the kids
after marriage, which caused me to hold on in ways that
were simply not healthy. I was terrified even to consider
the possibility that they would not be within reach if and
when I needed them. I thought they could kill the pain of
my loneliness. So, my fist grabbing on tightly, I looked to
them to meet my core longings.

Besides placing an unrealistic burden on others, this sets up you *and* them for frustration and disappointment. No human being (as we have seen) can meet the core needs of your life, nor were they ever meant to play such a role. Grabbing onto others because you think they can assuage your feelings of abandonment only kills relationships. It creates false intimacy based on selfishness and pretense, not the true intimacy that flows from perfect love. Henri Nouwen writes in *Reaching Out,*

> Friendship and love cannot develop in the form of anxious clinging to one another. . . . As long as our loneliness brings us together with the hope that together we no longer will be alone, we castigate each other with our unfulfilled and unrealistic desires for oneness, inner tranquillity and the uninterrupted experience of communion.
>
> p. 30

The closed-fist grabbing to hold others close because they temporarily still the storm within never brings peace. It simply feeds fear, because deep within you know that what you are depending on for life can be taken from you at a moment's notice. This reality has you scared to death. Imperfect love does that. Remember, perfect love drives out fear; imperfect love gives birth to fear!

The Aggressive Fist

The fist clenched in aggressiveness manifests itself in two ways. First, it is an imperfect love that demands, "You'd better give me what I want," and also, in great fear, it shouts, "Get away from me; I want nothing to do with you!" Let's look at each of these, beginning with the demand you place on others to come through or else.

Many people raise their fists to those they perceive to be threatening their own sense of peace. Take the abusive husband. His primary purpose in getting married was having someone there to meet his needs. He may be sensitive to some of his wife's needs, but most likely he is motivated by selfishness. As I heard one counselor say in a seminar, many aggressive men give love because they want something in return.

At some point the wife does not respond to him the way he wants. He begins to react in anger in an attempt to force her into compliance. Aggression levels may go all the way to physical abuse. In truth the man is insecure and afraid that his core needs will not be met. He may not be in touch with this fear, but it is there just the same. He has simply learned that, when threatened, he should make a fist and go get what he wants.

Men are not the only ones trapped in this kind of behavior. Women, though possibly less physical, can control husbands the same way. Words of blame, expressions of contempt and acts of punishment all represent an effort to say, "You're responsible to meet my needs, and since you haven't, take this!" Whether subtle or overt, these actions are meant to hurt and control spouses.

Why would anyone put up with this? Because he or she learned early in life that such attitudes and actions come with love. If you want the nurture, you take the abuse. It is all part of the same package. But as a result of playing the game, you are reinforcing the behavior. What is the answer? Choosing to find your fulfillment in the Lord and setting healthy boundaries that protect you from aggressive and domineering behavior, whether as victim or aggressor.

A second expression of the aggressive fist can be found when you defend yourself from others through anger. Whether through confrontation or silent withdrawal, the goal is the same: You want people to stay away from you. What do these responses have to do with love? They are an effort to protect you from people with the potential to hurt you.

On the one hand you clench your fist and push people away because they did not come through for you and you are bitter and resentful. Distance is your way of punishing them and declaring independence. It is rooted in fear and destructive to you and others.

On the other hand you warn people away with the clenched fist because you fear they are asking for something you are no longer willing to give. If you have maintained relationships by compromising yourself, you have learned to tuck away anything about yourself that may be unacceptable to those you need. But over time you begin to feel that you no longer know yourself since you have withdrawn to comply with the expectations of others. While you probably tolerate that withdrawal in some relationships, when one too many persons comes along, your defenses go up and you declare, "I've had it. You're not going to get one more piece of me." Your clenched fist is a warning that no one else is getting in; it is just too costly. Once again this aggressive fist response is based in fear.

The Resisting Fist

We face constant challenges in life, not least of which is the opportunity to grow and serve. Anyone who has followed the Lord for even a brief time knows that He does not allow us to rest in our comfort zones forever. He calls us to new places, new tasks and new levels of servanthood. If we are insecure in our relationship with the Lord, those changes can threaten what we define inappropriately as safety.

A scriptural definition of safety can be formed from Psalm 1. There the Lord advises us to stay connected with Him and with other believers, trusting that He is there to watch over us. Doing that, He promises, will keep us nourished and fruitful, like a tree planted by the stream—safe, as the Bible would define the term. What that text does not do is define safety as the absence of change or challenge or risk. Yet many of us fear these things because they threaten to reveal our weaknesses. We fear that we will fail, be unable to change or be overcome by something bad, and as a result be rejected. The result: coming face to face with our own sense of abandonment and loneliness. And that very thought causes us to say, "No, I won't go, I won't change, I won't accept that challenge."

For someone to lead you to a new place, you must reach out a hand and allow him or her to take you there. But if you have experienced humiliation and rejection because you were unsuccessful at trying something new, you may not want to be led into change and challenge and risk. So you clench your fist, dig in your heels, kick and fight and declare with intensity that you will not go! You may even throw false guilt into the mix, declaring that if God really loved you, He would not ask such a thing from you. If other people are connected to this call to change, you most likely resent and resist them as well. Your insecurity breeds fear—a sure sign that you neither trust God nor have confidence in yourself.

The resisting fist, like all these "fist" reactions, is a byproduct of imperfect love. Early on in life you failed, and as a result received some level of punishment—perhaps rejection, humiliation, ridicule or physical harm. Given your dark sense of abandonment and loneliness, this reaction paralyzed you with fear. At some point in the past you determined that you would never visit that horrible place again, and ever since your fist has been clenched against change, challenge and risk.

Only by pressing into God's perfect love will you be able to open your hand and allow Him to lead you into the place of growth.

The Fist of Control

We have already talked about control. It is a learned response aimed at keeping you from physical, emotional or relational harm. You have come to believe that the only way to get what you need is to take over the rudder and control the direction of your own life.

Maybe your approach is aggressive; possibly it is passive. You could be the kind of person who takes charge and gives orders to make sure everything turns out just the way you want. Conversely you may be the type who listens as others direct, only to do what you want, the way you want. Your tools might be manipulation or deception, or maybe you are the type who is upfront and open about what you expect. No matter what it looks like, the bottom line is the same: You have your hand tightly around the controls and have no intention of letting go.

Why do you do this? I am sure part of you wants to believe that you just like to see things done right. That way no one will be hurt or disappointed. Maybe so. But you also have a deep, gnawing fear that if things do not go as you want, you might be hurt, either through actual physical pain or through the heartache of rejection. You were, like everyone, loved imperfectly—most likely in a way that made you feel responsible for the well-being of yourself and others. You had to do it or no one else would.

So you have walked through life with your hand clenched around the controls. Probably you have become resourceful and successful at making your own way. Others may see you as a real leader. And you may be. But deep inside you feel all alone and responsible to make life turn out right. As a result you, like me, struggle with irrational and obsessive fear. It is only natural, for imperfect love does that, doesn't it?

God's Love Is All We Need!

When you have been the victim of imperfect love, you turn to express the same kind of relationship with others. You clench your fist and move through life deeply aware of

113

your own loneliness. You try to get what you feel you need, but you turn to people instead of God and try to be victorious, when the real answer is to surrender to His embrace.

Relationships built on imperfect love are invariably dependent ones. You and those around you try to get from each other what God alone can provide. Husbands, wives and friends all look to one another to make them feel important, secure and loved. The actions of "the other," you believe, determine your general peace and satisfaction.

But the suggestion that people are there to meet your needs is birthed in hell and leads only to great pain. Dependency in your life is linked singularly to God. Applying the term *dependent* to human relationships is absolutely and unqualifiedly dangerous! If you turn to people in this way, you will find not only that they let you down, but that you have given them power over your life that they should never have. In their imperfection they will end up, at best, disappointing you, or at worst, working you for their own purposes.

Deep inside you already know this is true, which in part is why you are in such a battle with fear. Imperfect love always does that to us. The time has come for you to reject it and all its unsatisfying ways of relating to yourself and others. God meant for you to walk in another way—the one founded on His perfect love.

Questions for Reflection and Review

1. In what way did the 1960s phrase *All you need is love* strike at the central issue of that day, and in what way did it miss the real need in people's lives?

2. John wrote in 1 John 4:18 that "perfect love drives out fear." What do you think he meant?

3. What did I intend to illustrate by the closed fist metaphor?

114

4. Why does imperfect love lead you to clench your fist in relationships?

5. What are the characteristics of imperfect love?

6. In what ways are you looking to people to be the source of your deepest needs? Why does that only engender more fear in your life?

7. What are two expressions of the aggressive fist? Are there ways in which you demonstrate this in relationships? If so, why?

8. Where do you tend to clench your fist in control?

9. What is meant by this statement taken from the chapter: "Applying the term *dependent* to human relationships is absolutely and unqualifiedly dangerous!"

10. Why should you seek to depend on God alone?

Perfect Love Does Drive Away Fear!

I have always been struck by the way the apostle John referred to himself in his gospel. He repeatedly called himself "the disciple whom Jesus loved." At first glance you might think he was being presumptuous or proud. The truth is, John was fully in touch with the Lord's great, passionate love for him, and he saw Jesus' love as the source of all he needed in life. John did not turn to others for these core needs. He was the beloved of the Son of God! As a result John was able to walk through a dangerous time with confidence and security. Even the days of imprisonment on Patmos did not shake his confidence. No matter how bad things appeared, John knew God was right there to bring good things to those He loved.

When John wrote his first epistle, he told his readers that what was true for him was equally true for all believers.

Under the inspiration of the Holy Spirit, John wanted his fellow Christians to know that they, too, were the beloved of God. Only the experience of divine love, he knew, satisfies the deep longings within us all:

> How great is the love the Father has lavished on us, that we should be called children of God! And that is what we are!
>
> 1 John 3:1

> This is how we know what love is: Jesus Christ laid down his life for us.
>
> 1 John 3:16

> This is love: not that we loved God, but that he loved us and sent his Son as an atoning sacrifice for our sins.
>
> 1 John 4:10

> God is love. Whoever lives in love lives in God, and God in him. In this way, love is made complete among us so that we will have confidence on the day of judgment, because in this world we are like him.
>
> 1 John 4:16–17

Each of these texts contains truths that are aimed straight at you. *You* are the beloved of God. It was for you that He sent Jesus to die on Calvary. You are the object of His great affection. God wants you to rest in His lavish and generous love. And, as it says in that last passage, God is love, and if you will only live in His love, you will be made complete. Complete! God, who is love, wants you to secure your very existence to His love as the source of all you need. His love contains everything you need to satisfy the cravings deep within your soul. His love is constant and eternal, never fading or passing away.

God's love for you is also unconditional. He does not give it because you act right nor take it away when you stumble into wrongdoing. His love is neither manipulative nor controlling. The Father does not lavish gifts on you so that you will in turn do Him a favor or meet a need. He has no needs, and loves you simply because it is His nature to be loving. You are His child, endowed with the very identity of Christ, heir to the Kingdom and graciously provided with every good thing from His hand. God longs for you to turn to Him, to come to know His love and to trust that through it you can find freedom, confidence, meaning and strength in this danger-filled life.

What else can I say? God delights over you and longs to hold you close to His heart. His love for you is immeasurable and unsearchable, able to bring light and life to the emptiness deep within your life. His love will chase away the feelings of abandonment and loneliness and fill you with peace—deep, lasting peace.

God's love, in other words, is perfect! It is the very source of all you need. And as you grow ever closer to His love, you will know that He will never take it away. As Paul wrote:

> I am convinced that neither death nor life, neither angels nor demons, neither the present nor the future, nor any powers, neither height nor depth, nor anything else in all creation, will be able to separate us from the love of God that is in Christ Jesus our Lord.
> Romans 8:38–39

What an incredible promise! You know about imperfect love—how conditional and manipulative and inconsistent and controlling it is. You have felt it your entire life, and all it has done is cause great fear. You have felt abandoned and alone when all you could do was grab onto a love that left you insecure and empty.

The time has come for you to learn more about God's perfect love.

- Soak in the truths of Scripture.
- Spend time meditating on God's promises.

119

- Declare the wonder of your new identity as His child.
- Come quietly into His presence and feel His intimate embrace.

Do that, and the dark place where fear has gained its power will become an interior castle of God's delight. His love will drive out irrational and obsessive fear, and you will learn to rest secure and at peace.

The Open Hand

When you live connected to God's perfect love, you approach relationships in an entirely new way. Whereas imperfect love drove you to clench your fist in fear, His perfect love will empower you to open your hand to others in peace and confidence.

As with imperfect love, I believe there are five manifestations of the open hand approach to relationships in life.

The Relaxed Hand

When you begin to move toward people out of God's perfect love, you will be able to relax in relationships. You will no longer be looking to people to meet your deepest needs. You will not be driven by fear to watch vigilantly for the slightest sign of disappointment or rejection. You will be increasingly confident of the Lord's acceptance, and link your identity to His great love. The anxiety will be gone and you will no longer fear that disapproval will open that dark box deep within your life. Your inner being will be filled with the Father's light and life. You will have found that He is all you really need.

While you will still want people to affirm what God has declared true in you, you will not need their affirmation as you did before. You will want to live in harmony with others, but their actions of acceptance or rejection will not be where you gain peace and security. God will have become enough for you, and fear will be driven from your life.

The Open Hand That Receives

At one time you felt that people had what you really needed to feel safe and secure. As a result you clenched your fist around what they offered and held it in a life grip, fearful that to let go meant darkness and death. But now, secure in God's perfect love, you will be able to keep your hand open. You will move into relationships without unreasonable demands, giving people room to relate to you, space to grow and freedom to love without condition or expectation.

As someone gives of himself to you, you will receive what he offers with joy, appreciating him for who he really is and hoping only the best for him. You will not smother him by demanding more, nor will you struggle to hold on when he can no longer give. His love and affection will be precious and deeply felt. Yet you will not expect him to fill your life or take away fear and loneliness. God almighty will be deep within, doing that work.

Time before the Lord will now fill your deepest need, enabling you to walk through life with your hand relaxed and open to others. You will be able to experience true communion and peace with your brothers and sisters, free from the driving pressures of unmet desires. You will be able to extend and receive love genuinely as Christ intended, without fear and anxious striving.

The Open Hand That Gives

Life for you used to be about getting. Your relationships were once important to kill pain and meet core needs. You often gave, but with an agenda to receive and secure what you needed from others. Many times you gave away parts

121

of who you really were, hoping such generosity would keep rejection and abandonment at bay. You would try to please others to gain even a crumb of acceptance. Doing this made you angry and bitter but you were too afraid to stop. With some people you could never say no, while with others you clenched your fist and said, "Don't even ask." Your approach to giving was unhealthy, hurting both you and others.

Now, embraced in the full love of God, you can give with a tender, open hand. You neither fear rejection, if what you offer someone is not enough, nor worry that your own needs will be compromised. God is the source for you. He will enable you to give even sacrificially without ever giving up what really sustains your life—His love. No matter how much you open your hand to share His love, you will always have more. There is enough—for you and for those you love—to last for all eternity.

Guilt will not motivate you anymore. You have been blessed, and now you will in turn be a blessing to others. It will be an easy yoke, and even in crisis a most pleasant calling. Because you have received from your Father, you will be able to give without condition or expectation. You will find no need to bully or blame, for fear will be gone, and in its place you will find peace.

The Hand Open to Be Led

When Jesus talked to Peter by the sea following the resurrection, He asked three times if Peter loved Him (see John 21:15–23). Jesus wanted to know if He held center stage in Peter's life and was all he needed. Peter responded three times that his love was there, though admittedly limited and still immature. With that Jesus told him that a day would come when Peter would be led to a place he did not want to go. Beyond a place of risk, Jesus was referring to Peter's persecution and death—a cross of crucifixion. He ended by saying to Peter, "You must follow me" (verse 22). Jesus would go before Peter to that place and provide what he needed on that day.

God does not promise you a risk-free or painless life. What He does assure you is that He will be there to provide what you need in that moment. Losses and separations and trials lie ahead. But resting in God's good love, you will be able to open your hand and allow Him to lead you through. His love will bring not only strength for the moment, but the assurance that even death will not separate you from the source of light and life. You will come to trust that good things are the result of that pilgrimage, for you and for others as well.

The Open Hand That Surrenders Control

For years you struggled to maintain control as a means of getting and keeping what you needed. Your methods may have worked in the short run, but the premise on which your actions rested was false. Control is an illusion, for the very nature of life involves risk and pain. No matter how tightly you grasped the rudder, the wind was always capable of shifting and blowing you right off course. Fear kept you clutching anxiously, while all the while you knew deep inside that the journey was ultimately beyond your control.

Now, by growing near to God and enjoying His sweet embrace, you will begin to loosen your grip on the rudder. You will grow to understand that the God who loves you controls even the wind that threatens to capsize your boat. While you do the possible, you will experience deep confidence that God is ever watchful and able to do the impossible. If He intervenes to keep you on course in the storm, great! If not, you trust that the wind of His Spirit is blowing you on a new course of His choosing. You will come to believe deep inside that the opposite of being in control is not being out of control, but resting in His control! As such your hand is ready to open at any time when He whispers, *I'll take it from here.*

The New Way of Perfect Love

The overall effects of perfect love are freedom and peace. Now you and your friends will be not dependent on one another, but connected to one another. No longer responsible for each other, you will instead become mutually accountable. Your love for one another will not strangle and wound but give life and room to grow. You will be able to bring healing and affirmation to your friends. And you will be patient with yourself and them, loving one another in an atmosphere in which you are all free to fail, to work through your weaknesses, and in vulnerability to confess your brokenness without judgment and condemnation. You will be able to give without an agenda, and the spirit of competition will be replaced with compassion and generosity. Your hand will be open, relaxed, free to give, to receive, to be led and to release control.

All this will be yours because you have been touched by perfect love. Fear will have been driven out and you will be at peace in God's secure embrace. You will become committed to a new way—one of confidence and deep trust in your Father's eternal love.

This transformation takes time. You need to grow closer to the Lord, to learn more about His provision for your life and to become increasingly aware of your new identity in Christ. These changes are all there for you, but you must reject the old way and choose the new way of approaching life.

In the following chapter I will share information and practical helps that will serve you in making this exciting transition.

Questions for Reflection and Review

1. Why do you suppose John referred to himself as "the disciple whom Jesus loved"?

2. What difference does such a self-concept make in a person's life? How would believing that affect your life on a day-to-day basis?

3. Reread the four passages from 1 John included on p.118. In what way are these relevant to your battle with fear?

4. What is the relationship between God's perfect love for you and your sense of safety and security in this risk-filled life?

5. What is the nature of God's unconditional love for you?

6. What is the relationship between God's unconditional love and your own deep sense of abandonment and loneliness? How does His love relate to that core need?

7. If you were resting secure in God's love, how would you change the way you relate to other people?

8. Why would you be able to open your hand to others if you were secure in God's great love?

9. How would that set you and others free and give space to grow?

10. What practical steps do you need to take in order to grow in your confidence in God's rich love?

Learning to Respond in a New Way

The way you have been responding to fear has not helped you. In fact, your reactions have increased the level of anxiety and worry in your life, causing you to grab all the more for control. More important, your method of managing fear has not addressed the core need in your life: getting reconnected with God. He alone has the answer to your deepest needs.

In this chapter I want to share some practical suggestions that will provide you with a new, healthier and more biblical way to meet the challenges of life. As a fellow pilgrim I would not offer this "new" way unless it really worked against irrational and obsessive fear! I never want to hear people's theories about overcoming problems unless what they are prescribing will actually help me. But I have found these steps practical and effective. If you will discipline yourself to embrace them as a new way of walking into fear, I am confident they will help you be an overcomer. Why? Because they are based on God's Word, applied specifically to the issues that lie beneath fear in your life.

Having said that, I am also concerned for you to realize that these practical steps must be built on the work we have already discussed. Our society is task-oriented, ever anxious to get the job done. Process means little to us, while we are almost obsessed with getting to the end result. I cannot overemphasize that such an attitude will not work in your struggle to overcome fear. If you embrace these steps without addressing what we have explored in the previous chapters, they will not work. Vulnerability, opening up to God for deep healing, renouncing all false premises and learning to soak in God's love must be the foundation on which you rest these biblical principles.

May I share a brief story to reinforce this critical point?

Emerging from the Dark

In 1979 I was appointed to pastor a small congregation in Western Pennsylvania. The church was located in Johnstown, the city devastated by flood in the late 1930s. Being there among those wonderful people was, without question, one of the best chapters of my life. My family joins me in looking back at those days with nothing but the warmest feelings of gratitude. The people were loving, generous and patient with a yet-unbroken and very young preacher!

The congregation was small when we arrived, affording me the opportunity to pastor the flock personally. I was able to spend time each week visiting from house to house, getting to know people in the church and care for their needs.

Eleanor and her son, Roger, attended our church faithfully. They were simple people, loving and extremely kind. I knew little about them other than the fact that

Eleanor's husband, Charles, never went to church and, years before, had been diagnosed with mental illness. Eleanor's brother, Dick, also a member of our church, had pretty much filled me in about Charles and left little doubt that he was probably uninterested in any help from the church. I took Dick's word for it and had no intention of trying to prove him wrong.

One day I went to see Eleanor and middle-aged Roger, who still lived at home. The three of us sat in the living room and had a great time getting to know one another. It did not even come to my mind to ask about Charles. I was there for Roger and Eleanor and focused all my attention on these two dear people. At one point in the conversation I mentioned that one of my pastimes included hunting. As I began to share a story, out of a darkened room to my right came these words: "I like hunting."

I was so startled that I was momentarily speechless. Charles had been sitting in that dark room listening to the entire conversation.

After an awkward silence I responded, trying to engage him more. Nothing. I did not hear another word all night.

Later, outside, Roger told me that his dad never came out when people were there. For years he had been unemployed, antisocial and heavily medicated. That he had spoken surprised even Roger.

After that night my thoughts were drawn back continually to Charles. That haunting voice from the darkness had stirred me, and I began to think of ways to draw him out again. First I took some hunting magazines over to his house, telling Eleanor they were especially for her husband. A week or so later I went back to visit, intentionally talking more about hunting and fishing.

Then I stopped by again to give Charles two pheasants I had bagged on a hunt, thinking he might like them for dinner sometime. As I presented them to Eleanor, telling her expressly that they were for Charles, he came out of the same room off the living room. He was a big man, much taller than I had anticipated, with thinning gray hair and large hands. He stood silently, stared for a moment, then came over and took them from Eleanor. Looking at me, he said thanks. Then he turned and walked back into the darkened room.

Breakthrough had occurred. Very soon Charles and I began to talk. After years of isolation, he was beginning to reconnect with another human being besides Eleanor and Roger.

Over time Charles and I began to share hunting stories and go for short walks. For the first time in years he was venturing outside his house. We became friends. Whenever I came to visit he would sit in the living room and participate in the conversation. In response to my patient questions, Charles would talk to me about his life, particularly his great fears and the pain of being outcast because of mental illness. His story was heartbreaking. Charles felt alone and deeply abandoned.

My involvement with Charles went on for almost two years. I kept inviting him to come to church. Frightened at first, he eventually came. After some time he met the Lord there and went on to join a Sunday school class for seniors with Eleanor. There were even times when, during class meetings, he played his trumpet. He grew to love being part of a larger family again. He was not without his eccentricities, but the people there accepted Charles lovingly into the group.

Eleanor's brother, Dick, exclaimed to me one day, "What you've done for Charles is a miracle!"

Certainly the Lord had touched Charles' life, but there was no miracle. Charles was changed by a very natural process used by the Lord. In fact, four simple ingredients led him into the arms of his heavenly Father. I spent *time* with Charles and *touched* a common chord by sharing his joys and sorrows. By doing that I was able to share the *truth* of God's love with him, and that helped him to *trust* the Lord more in his life. Time, touch, truth and trust.

Transformation will come into your life in no other way. The practical steps I am about to share will work if you are spending *time* before the Lord. You need to come before Him, both to work out your issues and to experience the power of His embrace. As you do, He will *touch* you in the joys and sorrows that come to you each day. You will learn that He cares deeply for you and is willing to help. The *truth* of His Word will become more a part of who you are, connecting you to your Father's strength and power, even when you feel weak and undone. After a while you will grow to *trust* Him more, realizing His commitment to bring good things into your life, even out of the toughest times.

The four ingredients of time, touch, truth and trust are simply a way of remembering and reinforcing what has already been said in the preceding chapters. You must invest in your relationship with the Lord on a regular basis before practical steps—like those I am about to share—will be effective in your life.

I advised you earlier that this is no quick-fix scheme but a long-term peace that comes by allowing the Lord to do a work far deeper than fear itself. If you try to shortcut the process, the forthcoming steps will be of little lasting help. But if you faithfully lay the foundation of time, touch, truth and trust, the principles that follow will work in your life. If you say yes to this work, I feel confident that what follows will help you respond to life and its challenges in a new and effective way. I encourage you to make the deeper investment for what promises to be a greater and more effective transformation deep within your life.

For the balance of this chapter I want to elaborate on one word among the four that is key to your life: *trust*. This concept is central to defeating the fear that continues to keep you locked in bondage and despair. When founded on *time*, *touch* and *truth*, *trust* holds the key to your freedom.

The Strategy to Help You Overcome Fear

One day as I was reflecting on all the Lord had been teaching me about overcoming fear, I realized that I kept coming face to face with the word *trust*. At first I thought, *Isn't that obvious? If I totally trusted the Lord, I would have no battle with fear.* But the more I considered the word, the more I realized it held a key to my own battle.

I spent an entire day prayerfully rehearsing that word and contemplating all that it meant. As I thought, I drew an acronym from the spelling of *trust* that would serve to guide me in facing life in a new way:

Think self-control.
Resist the urge to manage your pain.
Unload your concerns before the Lord in prayer.
Seek His presence in the midst of your trial.
Trust that He is committed to your good.

As I looked at this acronym, considering everything it was saying to me, I began to get excited. The Lord was showing me an entirely new way to respond when fear sought to overwhelm me. My old way had only broken me. But this new way held hope and promise that I would move forward against the irrational and obsessive fear that had held me captive for so long.

Whenever I want a concept to become second nature to me, I write it on my hand. So each and every morning I wrote the word *trust* on the palm of my hand. It served to remind me that this was the way to respond when I felt insecure and afraid. If panic started to arise, or the desire to avoid some challenge, or the temptation to react in control, I would turn to that acronym and ask the Lord to help me respond appropriately. I could sense new strength growing in me as I did so. And I have been using this acronym ever since to face the fears that still challenge my peace.

Let's look at the truth found in each of these five steps.

1. Think Self-Control

What normally happens when you find yourself in a potentially risky situation? Answer this question with particular reference to the places where irrational and obsessive fears arise within you. How do you feel at the time? What thoughts are you likely to have? What do you begin to do in response? Is your primary reaction to the situation a drive to gain control by some means? Even though your reaction may take place in a matter of seconds, there is unquestionably a pattern to your response.

Do you remember Summer's battle with fear? We identified the primary ingredients of a response sequence in her life that is quite common. Even if her case seems extreme, her issues illustrate the essential struggle we all have, regardless of the severity or frequency of our battles. Even problems with mild and less debilitating fears share a similar pattern. Let's briefly review that sequence, focusing on the irrational levels of fear Summer had about her children staying in the church nursery.

First, Summer, like all of us, was deeply afraid of abandonment and loneliness. One of the ways she killed this pain was through her children. While she may not have thought a great deal about the role they played in her life, it was true just the same. They were her deliverance from the awful darkness deep within her that threatened rejection, isolation and punishment. Having latched onto the kids as the primary source of her fulfillment, Summer fought desperately to keep them healthy, not just for their own well-being but also for her own.

Facing the possibility of their going into the church nursery, for example, Summer began to imagine every conceivable thing that might happen to hurt them. She considered every potential problem, regardless of how remote, taking it to its farthest conclusion. She visualized her children playing with toys, for example, that had been touched by a sick child. Then she imagined the kids catching the germ, coming home and getting ill with a severe fever. The doctor would be called, and she could hear him saying that the situation was quite serious. After picturing a traumatic hospital stay, she began to imagine the children not being there. The very thought brought great emptiness and pain.

All the while Summer's level of anxiety and fear grew higher and higher. She felt great distress, and the pain tapped into her own dark and frightening feelings of abandonment. So she raced to grab control of the situation. Eventually she landed on the idea that keeping the children out of the nursery was the only way to avoid this terrible disaster. This decision began to reduce her fear and pain. A semblance of peace came, and she had avoided a potentially horrifying situation. Summer had taken control, though her actions were driven by irrational fears that far outweighed the actual risk.

If you struggle with irrational fear, this scenario is familiar to you. It plays out in your own mind, too, although the sequence may occur subconsciously within a nanosecond of time. I could share these precise ingredients in describing my own battles, whether with flying, having a heart attack, being apart from my children or numerous other circumstances. When choosing the old way of responding, my mind obsesses, considering all the possibilities of risk; and as the fear level increases to painful levels, I grab for control. What you and I normally do does not help at all. The pattern simply reinforces fear and the darkness it feeds on deep within us.

My friend, there is another way for you to respond. It is the new, biblical and far healthier sequence that will enable you to overcome fear. The first step is for you to *Think self-control.*

Why Self-Control?

In my own pilgrimage toward freedom, I have searched the Scriptures regarding various issues related to fear. Do you know I have found no passage instructing me to gain control of the situation as a means of staying safe? Several admonitions in God's Word, on the other hand, call me to self-control in the face of risk.

In Peter's first epistle we find the apostle discussing trials and suffering. He says we will go through some very difficult days as Christians and goes on to assure us that God is ever close, that we have an eternal inheritance waiting for us in heaven and that God will use the fires of our trials to refine our faith, which is more precious than gold. Then Peter tells us what to do when facing a fearsome situation:

> Prepare your minds for action; be self-controlled; set your hope fully on the grace to be given you when Jesus is revealed.
>
> 1 Peter 1:13

Nowhere does he advise us to take on the full responsibility of the situation and grab control of it. Peter teaches, rather, that our minds are the real battleground and that we should keep them ready for action. Do not allow your thoughts to race away to wild scenarios of disaster. God's Word calls you to self-control!

Paul includes self-control as one of the fruits of the Holy Spirit's presence in your life (see Galatians 5:22–23). Ever

135

since you became a Christian, you have had the capacity for self-control. That includes control over your thoughts and actions. Granted, this ability may be vastly underdeveloped, but it is within you just the same. Your old way of responding involved a mind racing out of control and your desperate attempt to gain control of the situation. Now you are being encouraged to reject that sequence and begin a new pattern of response that begins with self-control.

How Does It Work?

You may be thinking that you cannot regain control of your racing thoughts (or whatever else might be out of control). On your own you are right. The flesh does not even want to respond like that! But the Holy Sprit is within you to help, and if you turn to Him, He will meet you in that moment. Remember what Paul said in 2 Timothy 1:7: "God did not give us a spirit of timidity, but a spirit of power, of love and of self-discipline." You have the capacity to respond to circumstances in the Spirit, who will empower you to gain self-control during the first moments when fear begins its assault. Let me illustrate.

Just the other day I was driving to a meeting where I was to speak. For the first time in almost a year, a feeling of panic began to come over me. Before, I might have reacted by stopping the car, turning around and driving home as quickly as possible. My mind would have raced to concoct all kinds of disastrous and irrational scenarios. Or at the very least I would have phoned a friend, asked him to meet me and travel with me to the appointment. But instead I chose to respond the other day in a new way. I prayed, "Lord, help me gain self-control. My mind is racing, and as a result I'm getting more and more frightened. Holy Spirit, take over my thinking, since Romans 8:6 tells me that 'the mind of sinful man is death, but the mind controlled by the

Spirit is life and peace.' I ask for Your help in controlling my mind, that I might have peace."

Friend, that is a prayer the Lord will answer, because it is in accordance with His Word. I felt God's empowerment, was able to move into peace and continue on to my appointment, where God ministered in power. Previously I had prayed that the fear would go away, that I would not die there by the road and all sorts of other desperate pleas. Now I simply begin with an appeal to help me gain self-control. And I have learned that He does hear that cry!

Praying for self-control in the moment of fear helps you in several ways. It keeps your mind from racing to irrational thoughts, which lead to controlling behaviors. It helps you remember that God is with you in the moment and that He loves you dearly. You are able to discern the true level of risk and respond accordingly. You can see what your responsibility is in the situation and what is beyond your control, resting that with the Father. I needed to keep my hands on the wheel as I drove to the appointment that day. That was clearly my responsibility. But not having a heart attack, not being hit by another car or not losing my mind were really beyond me. God was in control of that part of the journey; and by the Spirit's help I was able to surrender those concerns to Him and be at peace.

I know you will probably find this difficult at first. That is fine, for you have reacted inappropriately for years and it is not easy to undo an ingrained pattern. But as you take that first step to *Think self-control,* you will see that you are moving forward to freedom. The Lord will meet you in that moment and His presence will empower you to take the next step.

2. Resist the Urge to Manage Your Pain

Just the other day I had the opportunity to spend some time with a pastor going through a dark night of the soul.

In many ways the growth of the large, fast-growing congregation he shepherds is a tremendous success story. But, like many of us, James has been driven in ministry, which leads inevitably to breakdown. Depression and fear have become his companions and he is desperate for peace. Knowing that I had walked a similar journey, he called and asked to talk.

By God's grace I was able to relate to James' struggle and point him toward healing, particularly regarding the deep wounds fueling his workaholism. I shared my concerns about pursuing intimacy with the Lord and the richness that comes when we prioritize time with Him above all else.

James responded with thanks and we decided to get together again.

Then, as we were preparing to end our time together, he said, "You know, one of the most frightening times for me is in the middle of the night. I often wake up and a feeling of deep emptiness comes over me. It really frightens me. But I immediately begin to pray, 'Jesus, I love you, I really love you.' By repeating that over and over, I feel better and am able to get back to sleep."

My first thought was, *Why does he feel driven to tell that to Jesus at a time like that?* Hesitantly I asked him that question.

"I really don't know," James replied. "But it helps, and for me that's all that matters."

What this pastor was doing may have seemed spiritual and healthy to him. But the truth is, he was simply managing his pain. By praying he was no different from someone who turns on the television, calls a friend, takes a sleeping pill or goes to the refrigerator for a snack or binge. Granted, he was not turning to alcohol or drugs or finding an improper sexual outlet, but he was still taking an anesthetic designed to numb the pain of emptiness and fear.

You have your own painkillers, and in your old way of responding turned to them for quick relief. Most likely there was a compulsive element to your behavior, not unlike James' repetitious prayer. You would "do" something over and over until the fear went away. Sometimes what you did seemed acceptable, like checking the door several times at night to make sure it was locked. Other behaviors may have seemed less rational, like washing your hands constantly. Either way the goal was eliminating the pain of deep fear.

The problem with this behavior is that it never addresses the core issues that fuel the fear. You are simply finding a way to manage fear, not overcome it. The lasting solution is facing the fear, not killing it. Irrational and obsessive fear is really an alarm sounding off in your life, signaling that something is very wrong inside. All you do by using a compulsive behavior to numb your feelings is turn off the alarm. Fear is sending you a message, and you are responding by killing the messenger! Such behaviors do nothing about the destructive fire consuming you deep inside.

Don't manage your fear; embrace it and find out what lies beneath it. You will find that God will meet you there and guide you to new life.

I advised my pastor friend to try a new approach. Instead of killing his fear that came out of emptiness, I encouraged him to be open and honest about it and ask God to meet him there.

What James discovered changed his life. He told me that the very next night, when he awakened to the same emptiness and fear, he went out to the couch and sat there allowing the feelings to surface. As before, a deep sense of emptiness swept over him. But instead of trying to eliminate the feeling, he asked the Lord to meet him there and be his help. In the midst of his struggle, James told me, he heard the Lord whisper deep within his spirit, *You feel empty inside because you are empty. Come to me and I will meet you and fill your life with My presence.*

Something changed that night, this pastor told me, and he told me he was going to seek God's presence above everything else in his life. Instead of managing fear, he had learned to face and embrace it, and he found the Lord right there to help him overcome it.

The prophet Isaiah identified two ways to handle darkness:

> Let him who walks in the dark, who has no light, trust in the name of the LORD and rely on his God. But now, all you who light fires and provide yourselves with flaming torches, go, walk in the light of your fires and of the torches you have set ablaze. This is what you shall receive from my hand: You will lie down in torment.
>
> Isaiah 50:10–11

Your managing behaviors are nothing but torches that you light in order to chase away the darkness of fear. All they will ever bring is torment. But walk into the darkness of fear and you will find God there to give you the treasure of His wonderful love and peace. He will meet your deepest needs and bring life and light to your life. Remember, *Resist the urge to manage your fear.* Allow the Lord to touch you and set you free.

Now it is time to take another step forward along the new way.

3. Unload Your Concerns before the Lord in Prayer

Given your old, aggressive way of reacting to fear, you may feel that what I am suggesting does nothing to help you deal with the perceived or actual risk. After all, if you are facing a genuinely life-threatening illness, for example, what do self-control and resisting the urge to manage the fear of death really do about the problem?

It may feel at this point that you are simply putting your head into the sand and ignoring the problem. The truth is, you are now positioning yourself to respond to your situation in a healthy, balanced way. You are centering on God's presence, and from that foundation you are now ready to move toward Him in concerted prayer.

The Lord does not want you to deny the level of risk in your circumstances or pretend that everything is fine when it is not. He invites you to come in prayer and lay out your feelings, concerns and desires before Him. He wants you to tell Him about your fears and petition Him for help and relief.

Look at Jesus—He did that very thing on the night of His betrayal and arrest. Jesus and His disciples went to Gethsemane following the Last Supper. There He went before His Father in prayer, seeking His help regarding the coming hours of suffering. Jesus did not sugar-coat the situation, pretending everything was fine. First He told His followers that He was "overwhelmed with sorrow to the point of death" (Mark 14:34). Then, considering His impending rejection, suffering and separation from God, He asked His Father to take the cup of suffering away if at all possible. Three times He asked God to find another way. Jesus was open and vulnerable before God, unleashing His emotional upheaval and concern. Once He had done this, however, He rested the entire matter with His Father and said, "Not what I will, but what you will" (verse 36).

This account provides us with a wonderful model for addressing our own concerns. Go to God and tell Him about your fears. Pour out your emotional turmoil before Him without putting a pretty face on your feelings, following the advice of King David: "Trust in him at all times, O people; pour out your hearts to him, for God is our refuge" (Psalm 62:8). Ask the Lord for His help, being honest about your specific hopes for the situation. Ultimately, if you come humbly and honestly, you will break through to His presence and find peace. You will not necessarily hear Him promise to do as you ask, but you will know that He has heard you and that He will be there for you. You will be able to surrender to His will and come into His rest.

Paul provides a helpful model for such prayer in his letter to the Philippians:

> Rejoice in the Lord always. I will say it again: Rejoice! Let your gentleness be evident to all. The Lord is near. Do not be anxious about anything, but in everything, by prayer and petition, with thanksgiving, present your requests to God. And the peace of God, which transcends all understanding, will guard your hearts and your minds in Christ Jesus.
>
> Philippians 4:4–6

Are you able to see the elements of your new pattern of response in this admonition? You are self-controlled, your thoughts focused on the nearness of Christ and the goodness of God in a spirit of rejoicing. Instead of acting out of nervous anxiety, you are approaching the issue gently and thankfully. You are then able to lay out your prayers before the Father, telling Him specifically about your desires, feelings and concerns. Paul promises that peace will result in your mind and heart.

Decide right now that the next time you are struggling, instead of rushing to find some way to silence the pain: *Unload your concerns before the Lord in prayer.*

I went through a season of anxiety so intense that I considered being medicated to find relief. At times that is advisable, but I clearly sensed the Lord calling me to another way. So each and every time anxiety hit, I went to the Lord and talked to Him about it. I asked Him to show me the roots, strengthen me for the battle and take away the problem. I did this for several months. Two things happened. First, I grew to know the Lord much better because

I was praying so often! Second, He did a deeper work than simply to still the storm of my fear. He went to the roots beneath fear and brought deliverance and cleansing. Anxiety did not leave me immediately. But it drove me to God for an even more vital work deep within my life.

Let me encourage you, then, to turn to God with three different kinds of prayer. First, go ahead and talk to Him, telling Him everything about your need. List all your concerns in their full description. Then move on to dialogue with God. Don't just talk *to* Him; communicate *with* Him. Ask for direction and revelation, taking time to listen. Let prayer be a two-way exchange, a give-and-take of deepening relationship. Be silent for extended periods, waiting to hear His whispers in your own spirit. Finally, simply soak in His presence in a spirit of adoration. Choose some aspect of God's character, such as His love, on which to meditate; then worship and give thanks simply and quietly. Don't talk; just commune with Him. Picture yourself leaning on His breast, feeling the comfort of His nearness and tender embrace. Say nothing and do not try to hear something from Him. Just be with Him for a good while.

This third level of prayer will transform you in the deepest regions of your inner being. It is where the real victory over fear truly begins!

4. Seek His Presence in the Midst of Your Trial

One day I was taken aback by a woman in the book section of a discount warehouse in California. She had a book open and was bringing it right up to her nose, then moving it slowly away from her face, staring at the page the entire time. She did this several times. My curiosity aroused, I moved in for a closer look. Then I saw that she was holding a book of Japanese three-dimensional art. At first glance the page looked like nothing but a psychedelic collection of geometric shapes. But when viewed from a particular angle, with a particular focus of the eyes, a three-dimensional picture would become visible. Whatever the text had told this woman was there in the picture, she was not going to give up until she found it!

Your heavenly Father is ever present in the challenges of life, even in the midst of darkness and fear. If you are intent on finding Him in these times, you will come to a new level of relationship with Him. Too often you are singularly focused on finding a way to control the situation and ease your pain. Change your goal and look first to find Him right there with you. Your encounter in His presence will make the risk of the situation less intimidating. Once having found God there, you will experience new peace and His strength made perfect in weakness.

When I first entered my own dark night of the soul, crushed by depression and agoraphobia, I had (as I said early on) but one goal—getting out of there as quickly as possible! Nothing I did, however, sped up the healing. So I turned to another improper goal: If I could not get out fast, what could I do to kill the pain? That attitude did not help either. Finally I read Jean Pierre de Caussade's eighteenth-century classic, *The Sacrament of the Present Moment* (HarperCollins, 1989) and was led to seek God more than healing in the situation. This approach changed my life. The depression and agoraphobia continued to debilitate me for a season and were very painful. But the Lord met me in the darkness and I felt His embrace as never before. I learned there was something more important than the relief of pain. I discovered God in a way I had never known.

David wrote, "Even though I walk through the valley of the shadow of death, I will fear no evil, for you are with me; your rod and your staff, they comfort me" (Psalm 23:4). What was true for David is equally true for you. The Lord is with you right in the middle of your pain and trial. He is ever present at your side in the moment of risk. Find Him there and rest secure in His love. If He deems it best, He will use His rod to defeat your enemies. At other times He will use His staff to lead you to a better place with Him. It may not feel that good at first, but in time you will come to see that He has your very best in mind.

Two stories from Scripture have transformed my understanding of the Lord's presence in trouble. The first is the familiar account of when King Nebuchadnezzar made an image of gold and commanded every subject of his kingdom to bow before it. Three Israelite boys refused and as a result were sentenced to death in a furnace of fire. They declared:

> "The God we serve is able to save us from it, and he will rescue us from your hand, O king. But even if he does not, . . . we will not serve your gods or worship the image of gold you have set up."
>
> Daniel 3:17–18

Into the furnace they went. But instead of dying there, they met the Lord in a miraculous way. He actually walked in the fire beside them, and in the end they were delivered from an awful death. They had not put their trust in God's willingness to keep them from harm. They had trusted, rather, that regardless of the outcome, God would be there with them. Can you imagine the story the young men told after that encounter? I am sure it was far more about the glory of the Lord in the moment than the heat of the fire! They met God in the trial and were saved.

The second story that has transformed my understanding of God's presence in trouble is that of the stoning of Stephen. Brought before the religious leaders of Jerusalem, the apostle gave a stirring testimony of God's faithfulness to Israel. He rebuked them for rejecting Christ, and at one moment was so caught up in the Spirit that he saw Christ standing at the right hand of God (see Acts 7:55–56). Furious, the elders stoned Stephen to death as he spoke gentle words of forgiveness. Once again we see that in the moment of trial, the Lord was not off preoccupied with other matters. He was right there, standing to act on Stephen's behalf and actually open heaven before him. Unlike the three Israelite boys in the furnace, Stephen was not delivered from death. But God was there all the same, strengthening him to walk through the suffering and into His eternal Kingdom.

When fear assails you, look for the Lord in the middle of the moment. Seek His presence and rest in His arms of love. He will be there. Possibly He will remove the burden of your trial and pain. But maybe He will not, strengthening you instead to move through it to an entirely new place with Him. Either way you will know Him better than you have before. And the fears that have kept you locked in obsessive efforts to control your world will be driven out by His perfect love.

The writer of Hebrews promises that God "rewards those who earnestly seek him" (Hebrews 11:6). Instead of trying anxiously to find a way out, *seek His presence in the midst of your trial.* You will find Him there and never be the same!

5. Trust That God Is Always up to Good Things on Your Behalf

You know that life is a risky proposition with no guarantee that people will not face trial and suffering. That is part and parcel of the human experience. What frightens you, however, is the reality that "bad" things (as you would define *bad)* happen even to good people. Christians come face to face with deep heartache. They experience loss, violence, debilitating illness, even death. Knowing this brings the stark realization that you are not immune just because you have received the Lord into your heart. In fact, considering the possibilities can create great fear that something bad will happen to *you*. So you try to grab control as a way of reducing the risk, thus eliminating the fear of potential harm. The core problem is that your trust in God is incomplete, and as a result you do not experience His rest, even in the midst of pain and suffering.

Many Christians would have you believe that the Lord never allows His children to suffer if they have sufficient faith in Him. Just the other day I was thumbing through a leading Christian magazine and saw a full-page ad for an upcoming conference featuring a popular charismatic evangelist. The ad included a quote from the speaker telling people that God wants us healthy, prosperous and successful. He assured potential conference-goers that he would give them principles to follow to help them get in touch with God's provision.

Rather than get excited by this promise, I was saddened. Such claims are inconsistent with the full counsel of God's Word. I know Psalm 91 as well as the next person and have found comfort in its promise of God's protection and care for His own. God knows the number of hairs on my head and will care for me with even more affection than He does the sparrows. But I have sat with Christians convinced He would never allow them to suffer, only to be undone by an unexpected season of darkness. They are often angry at God because He was unfaithful to what they saw as His promise to keep them safe. Had they done something wrong to anger Him? Was evil just more powerful than God, assaulting His children while He stood by impotent, unable to do anything about it? Or should they now assume responsibility because their faith was insufficient and carry the blame?

I am convinced that our definition of care does not always match God's. As a result we impose upon Him expectations that are just not consistent with the Scriptures. Romans 8:28–29 is instructive on this point:

> We know that in all things God works for the good of those who love him, who have been called according to his purpose. For those God foreknew he also predestined to be conformed to the likeness of his Son, that he might be the firstborn among many brothers.

This passage is clear about the ultimate good purpose God has for your life: He wants you to grow more and more like Jesus. How does He move you toward that transformation? Paul said He uses "all things." Do you hear that? All things! Yes, God is deeply committed to your well-being and joy. But the Scripture is clear that there are times He allows suffering and loss to come your way. And the Bible is equally intentional about telling you that such trials develop your relationship with the Father to a deeper level. Look at the following passages:

> We rejoice in the hope of the glory of God. Not only so, but we also rejoice in our sufferings, because we know that suffering produces perseverance; perseverance, character; and character, hope. And hope does not disappoint us, because God has poured out his love into our hearts by the Holy Spirit, whom he has given us.
>
> Romans 5:2–5

> Consider it pure joy, my brothers, whenever you face trials of many kinds, because you know that the testing of your faith develops perseverance. Perseverance must finish its work so that you may be mature and complete, not lacking anything.
>
> James 1:2–4

In this you greatly rejoice, though now for a little while you may have had to suffer grief in all kinds of trials. These have come so that your faith—of greater worth than gold, which perishes even though refined by fire—may be proved genuine and may result in praise, glory and honor when Jesus Christ is revealed.

1 Peter 1:6–7

These are but a few of numerous texts that tell you: *God is always up to good things on your behalf,* even in the midst of difficult and frightening times. As you look to Him in trust, He may deliver you as He did the three Israelite youths, or He may allow you to walk through the dark night as a means of perfecting you into the image of Christ. Either way He will be there with you, up to something good in your life!

I would never have thought that depression and agoraphobia were conditions I would bless! But I want you to know that I do. Walking through that trial has changed me and transformed my relationship with the Lord. I have not arrived, by any means. But those days pressed me into God as nothing else had done. Whereas once I cursed those days as a time of great pain, now I bless them as a season of transformation.

My dark hour is nothing compared to what others have walked through. Consider Dave Dravecky. An All-Star major league pitcher with the San Francisco Giants, he enjoyed financial reward and the adulation of fans. He was living the dream of almost every man and boy in America. But all this came to an end when he developed cancer in his throwing arm. He had to have his arm amputated, which ended his career. I was overwhelmed when I read in his autobiography *Comeback* (Zondervan/HarperSanFrancisco, 1990) about the suffering he endured. He battled emotional and physical pain that was intense and debilitating.

149

What was his ultimate reaction to this season? In his second book, *When You Can't Come Back* (Zondervan / HarperSanFrancisco, 1994), Dave wrote:

> When I look back over the past four years and see all I've learned from other people who have suffered, all I've experienced of other people's love, all God has shown me of His mercy and comfort, all the encouragement my small measure of suffering has given to others, I think: *If I'd continued on as a ballplayer and missed that, now that would have been a tragedy.*
>
> p. 195, emphasis added

Dave Dravecky is able to see that God is always up to something good. It may not look like that in the middle of the darkness, but it is true just the same. Does that mean a person who believes this way never feels afraid? No, fear will come in as before to assault you, threatening harm and abandonment. But as you lean on the testimony of Scripture and your ever-deepening relationship with the Lord, trust takes over where fear once reigned. You begin to rest in the fact that, whether you are delivered from the trial or given the strength to go through it, your heavenly Father is up to something very good in your life. He is drawing you close in His embrace and conforming you to the very nature of His Son. You will be able to declare with the psalmist, "Before I was afflicted I went astray, but now I obey your word. You are good, and what you do is good" (Psalm 119:67–68).

Choose This New Way!

I am still a pilgrim on the journey to freedom and wholeness. In some places the light of God's love has driven away the fear that once held me captive. In other areas the work continues as I battle to embrace the darkness that threatens to undo me. I must say no to my past desire to be in control, choosing to respond with ever deepening levels of *T-r-u-s-t.*

You, too, can choose this new way. The Lord waits to meet you as you walk away from old patterns and into His arms of perfect love. Write the truths of the *T-r-u-s-t* acronym on your heart and turn there each time fear issues its challenge. I believe you will soon be celebrating more areas of newfound strength and freedom in your life! You will be enjoying increased peace and the joy of knowing that God is transforming you into a mighty overcomer.

Questions for Reflection and Review

1. Remember back to the story of Charles. What process helped him move beyond fear to increasing levels of freedom?

2. Parallel Charles' growth with your relationship with God. How could you experience the same process in growing closer to Him?

3. What does the acronym *T-r-u-s-t* stand for?

4. What is the difference between self-control and seeking to be in control?

5. In what ways do you try to manage your fears?

6. Why is it so important that you not do that?

7. How did Jesus address His great despair in the Garden of Gethsemane? What does that teach you about dealing with your own fears and concerns?

8. Why is it important that you seek the Lord's presence in the midst of trials? In what ways will He meet you there?

9. What is similar about the story of the three boys in the furnace and the stoning of Stephen? What is different? What do these accounts teach you about fear?

10. Reread Romans 8:28–29. What is Paul telling you?

A Word about Panic

In the spring of 1992 my son Aaron accompanied me on a weeklong trip to Nyack, New York. We had lived there previously and I was returning to teach an intensive course at the seminary where I had been on faculty. Aaron, then a teenager, went along to spend time with his old buddies. We were both excited about being back in the East and made the most of our week there. I taught all day, enjoying the interchange with the students and spending great time with my friends and colleagues. Aaron played basketball every day and enjoyed his friends immensely. He and I ate pizza almost every evening, "batching" it together and having a ball.

But I had arrived in New York already experiencing signs of burnout. It had been an extremely busy time at home before we left and I felt drained. During our week in New York I had to lecture for 42 hours in five days. By the third day I was running on pure adrenaline. I pushed through my fatigue, however, and gave the students everything I had. When the course ended on Friday, I was exhausted but satisfied that the class had been a success.

That evening I went over to a colleague's home for dinner. I felt uneasy and anxious as I arrived and found it difficult to stay focused on the conversation. A thought came to me: Maybe something more than fatigue was going on. Suddenly, with the force of a locomotive, I began to panic. My heart began to race uncontrollably, I grew lightheaded, I felt as if I could not get my breath and I broke out in a sweat. Never had I experienced anything like this! I left the room immediately and ran outside for air. My friends followed, surprised and concerned. I stood for a moment trying to calm down but only grew more frightened. I told them I just had to leave, and if I felt better later I would come back.

Making my way to the apartment where Aaron and I were staying, I went inside to find him. He was not there and I grew more frightened. Going back out, I walked the campus looking for him everywhere, afraid I was having a heart attack and desperately wanting him with me. But I could not find him anywhere. Returning to the apartment, I paced the floor, terrified. I decided to lie down but that lasted about a minute. *Maybe if I get a shower,* I thought, *I'll feel more relaxed.* No way! It did not touch the fear I was experiencing. Finally I called a friend on faculty who was a psychologist. He came over immediately and helped me calm down. He knew about panic attacks and talked me gently through the fear to a reasonable state of relaxation.

Afterward I was unsure about what had just happened. I had battled fear for years but never panic like this. I was terribly frightened and wondered what else might be lurking around the corner to get me. Because this experience had hit me without warning, my entire sense of control had been blown to bits.

The truth is, I can see in hindsight that symptoms had been there for some time—symptoms I ignored or numbed from my conscious mind through some painkiller. But this episode respected none of my coping mechanisms, blowing right through them to undo me. What followed was a yearlong battle with severe panic disorder, and then a several-year process of relearning and rebuilding.

Initially I thought that this panic attack was the worst thing that had ever happened to me. I felt ashamed, humiliated and concerned that my entire life was being turned upside down in the most disastrous way! I also thought I was losing my mind, which only fueled the panic.

Following the New York incident I began to experience more panic attacks. They occurred in church, at the store, in restaurants, driving the car and countless other places. That is when I started to fear having a heart attack—a common reaction to this kind of problem. Soon, in order to find peace, I began to retreat from the world. Depression increased and I found it almost impossible to cope. It was a very dark time for me. I was convinced that my career was done for and I wept deeply that my children had to see me struggling. Life, I thought, was essentially over. Eventually I had to get professional help to regain a sense of balance.

Now I see that my struggle to overcome panic attacks helped me get to the roots of some important issues in my life. Today (as I said in the last chapter) I am thankful to have walked that path. The combined season of depression and panic disorder actually redefined my life in the best possible way.

The good news for anyone battling a similar condition is that it is definitely a winnable fight. The Lord has enabled me to reclaim most of the ground lost during those days. More importantly He has brought me to a much deeper place with Him and to a far more balanced and pleasurable approach to ministry. The season in the dark also birthed within me a concern for broken people and a willingness to share my own story when it can help others find the Lord in a new way.

With God's help I have been able to walk a long ways down the path to freedom, and I want to share what I learned with you.

What Is Panic Disorder?

Everyone experiences moments of anxiety and panic. But when these natural responses begin to alter your patterns of life, they have moved toward becoming a disorder.

Panic attacks are essentially seasons of intense anxiety that produce some kind of physical reaction—perhaps a racing heart, sweating, breathing difficulties, upset stomach, depression, sleeplessness or chest pain. Many people who have battled panic attacks admit fears about losing their minds, having a heart attack, being out of control and obsessing about sudden death. The level and intensity of panic attacks, as with all such problems, vary from person to person. But regardless of the severity, these attacks take a deep psychological toll and limit a person's joy and freedom in life.

I am no expert on panic disorder, simply a fellow traveler sharing some thoughts that may bring help and hope to a struggling brother or sister. There are numerous books and programs that are expansive and quite helpful. I always recommend one book to my friends, *From Panic to Power* by Lucinda Bassett (HarperCollins, 1995). Lucinda Bassett was practically homebound as a result of panic and anxiety. After battling back to freedom, she helped found the Midwest Center for Stress and Anxiety and has developed a successful program to help people struggling with these problems. Lucinda Bassett is also a Christian and links faith in Christ to her healing and recovery. I recommend her work to you wholeheartedly for a more thorough treatment of this topic.

Here I want to share some basic information that will help you move toward greater freedom in your life. What follows are ten suggestions that will help you overcome this frightening problem. They have worked for me and I am sure you will find them helpful for your own journey. But before moving to these steps, let me assure you of two important truths.

First, the Lord is with you in the midst of this struggle. Allow this season to take you to a new level of relationship with Him. Nothing is more important in your life. Intimacy with God is even more important than overcoming your problem with panic. In fact, I challenge you to offer this season to the Lord as a vehicle to bring you closer to Him than you ever dreamed possible. Find the Treasure hidden in this dark night. I assure you, He is there waiting to hold you tight! Allow your struggle with anxiety and panic to be part of the "all-things" strategy of your heavenly Father. If you do, you will find that what the evil one hoped to use to break you will actually become a tool of the Lord to transform your life!

Second, this battle is winnable! You are not locked into a mental disorder and destined to live this way the rest of your life. Although there are physical components to your problem, this is primarily a battle in your mind. Your own patterns of thinking are fueling your struggle. With the Holy Spirit's help, it will be your thinking that enables you to overcome debilitating panic. I did not believe that at first but came to know that it is the truth. There is nothing but hope for you in this battle so long as you are willing to lean into the Lord and do the work. I know many people who used to live in absolute bondage (much as I did) who are living today with joy and excitement. So take heart.

The following ten suggestions will help you move closer to God and ultimately enable you to overcome this problem.

1. Address the Core Issues in Your Life

Any number of books about panic and anxiety focus on helping you change your thinking patterns and behaviors as a way of overcoming fear. Certainly these are important issues and must be addressed. But beneath the panic are core wounds that have caused much of the problem in the first place. Allow me to remind you once again that you must do more than simply modify your behavior; you must go to the root.

Patterns of fear and panic can be traced to wounds that occurred early in your life. Possibly you were raised in an angry, aggressive environment. Maybe your parents were alcoholics, and to survive you had to reverse roles and take care of them. Many who experience panic come from homes in which parents were critical, highly demanding or downright impossible to please. Maybe you are one of countless individuals who were abused physically or sexually. Or perhaps your parents distanced themselves from you when you did wrong, communicating that failure leads to abandonment and loneliness.

Whatever the specific pattern, such wounds affect your life and are very likely related to any battles with fear and panic. Lasting change takes place only when these core issues are addressed. Refer to chapter 5 for a detailed discussion of this process. It is enough here simply to remind you of these steps and to encourage you once again to do the work. Opening yourself to deeper healing requires that you:

1. Embrace the darkness within your life, asking the Lord to reveal the wounds that lie beneath your fear.

2. Grieve the losses that occurred as a result of those wounds.

3. Receive an infusion of God's truth.

4. Pursue intimacy with God above all else.

5. Connect with a caring community.

If you move carefully through this process, especially with the help of a spiritual director, counselor or trusted friend, you will be going far deeper than the behaviors that relate to your panic and fear. You will be opening yourself to God's healing touch right where the fear gains its power—at the core wounds within your life. You can then move on to embrace the suggestions that follow from a foundation that will support the kind of lasting change you desire.

2. Pay Attention to Spiritual Realities

The apostle Paul admonished the Christians in Ephesus to "be strong in the Lord and in his mighty power" (Ephesians 6:10). Then he warned them that the battle we face in the world is not relegated exclusively to what we can see, feel, hear and touch:

> Our struggle is not against flesh and blood, but against the rulers, against the authorities, against the powers of this dark world and against the spiritual forces of evil in the heavenly realms.
>
> verse 12

Could it be that there is a spiritual component to your battle with fear? My answer is a qualified yes. I do not believe there is a demon behind every bush, nor do I embrace the idea that the devil is the cause of every problem in your life. Satan is active, however, to steal, kill and

159

destroy, as Jesus warned in John 10:10. He may well seek to use your problem with fear and panic to his advantage.

Where is the battle with fear really fought? Primarily, I believe, in the mind, and the evil one is not above attacking your mind with threats and suggestions of wild scenarios of harm to get at you. You do well to realize this and follow the biblical instructions regarding combating Satan's evil schemes.

Paul went on to urge the Ephesian Christians to put on the full armor of God against evil and to pray in the Spirit on all occasions (see Ephesians 6:13–18). Elsewhere he wrote that believers must wage war against the devil by "[taking] captive every thought to make it obedient to Christ" (2 Corinthians 10:5). Paul also admonished his readers to "be transformed by the renewing of [their] mind[s]" (Romans 12:2).

What is the point? Do not fail to take the spiritual dynamics of your struggle into consideration. Do as Paul tells you and put on the armor of God in prayer each day. Pray in the Spirit, seeking the Lord's help in your battle to walk free of panic and fear. Ask the Holy Spirit to help you take every thought captive, making it obedient to Christ. Guard your mind with the defenses of the Lord, thinking on the good and powerful truths of His Word.

I am not suggesting that your struggle is nothing more than demonic attack. There is more to it than that. But the evil one seeks to capitalize on that problem, using it as ground for an assault against you. Be alert to his ways, therefore, and wise enough to pay attention to these spiritual realities. Remember, the closer you draw to God in your life, the more peace you will experience.

3. Get a Thorough Medical Checkup

If you have not done so recently, get a thorough physical from your doctor. It will help you put your concerns into perspective. You may be one of those people who obsess about their health, particularly when battling seasons of panic. I have already indicated that I used to do this, imagining all sorts of possibilities. Was I going to have a heart attack? Did I have a brain tumor? Was cancer growing deep inside my body? When I was struggling with panic, these and countless other worries were always gnawing at my mind. If you do this, too, the best thing you can do for yourself is get a physical. It will help reduce the fuel for fear within your mind, enabling you to put your energies where they really belong to overcome this problem.

A second reason for a physical is to receive a doctor's assessment of your general health. Long battles with panic and anxiety put stress on your system, causing some side effects at times that need attention. Your doctor will be able to assess this and help you move to better health. My doctor ran tests for a possible tumor on my adrenal gland. In rare cases, he said, panic is a side effect of that problem. The results were negative, as he predicted, but it was important that he find out through proper testing. Have a good checkup, then, to stay on top of your health at a time when panic is weighing heavily on your mind.

A third reason for a thorough physical is to address body chemistry issues. It may be that anxiety and panic are bringing about an imbalance in your chemical makeup, and as such you find it difficult even to cope in life. If so, certain medications may help you get stabilized so you can address the issues fueling panic. Many Christians struggle with the idea of medication for emotional and mental problems. This is unfortunate, for proper medication can help when you are battling panic and anxiety, especially to the degree that your life has been radically altered by the disorder.

My advice: Get a doctor's opinion. Personally I am uncomfortable with taking medicines to mask anxiety and panic. They are a tool used best, I believe, in support of the deeper work needed in a person's life. Addressing core wounds and changing patterns of thinking and behavior will have a profound effect on your body chemistry. These changes are the best medicine you can ever give yourself.

4. Pay Attention to Diet, Vitamins and Exercise

Don't you hate it when someone who previously struggled with a problem suddenly becomes fanatical about that very health issue? Well, watch out, because I am now that person!

Until my breakdown the only guideline I observed was, "Do I like what I am about to eat?" If the answer was yes, I indulged. I ate candy regularly and drank two or three sodas almost every day. I told my students I could be bribed with chocolate chip cookies and almond chocolate bars, and kept a desk drawer in my office dedicated to both. Depression and anxiety forced me, however, to take a hard look at these excesses. My system was very sensitive, I learned, to both sugar and caffeine, responding with seasons of anxiety and then swings into mild depression. Because I was ill enough at the time to do anything, I eliminated all caffeine, chocolate and most processed sugars from my life.

It has now been five years, and for me there is no looking back. The improvement in my mood swings and anxiety levels has been significant. While I still struggle from time to time with situational anxiety, the chronic sense of nervousness and tension are long gone. At first eliminating caffeine and sugar from my diet was hard, but after about three months all cravings disappeared, and I really do not miss these foods at all.

I encourage you to seriously consider the relationship between diet and anxiety and make the necessary changes. In a short time you will feel the effects and be glad you did.

If you are prone to anxiety and panic, be careful about the use of alcohol as well. Many people self-medicate this way and it can lead to serious problems.

You will also find that taking vitamins regularly will help you, as will some daily exercise. Both of these commitments help your body chemistry. Every day I take a B-complex vitamin, which I believe has contributed to my general health and increased my energy level significantly. I also find that a daily walk enables me to unload stress and increase my overall sense of well-being. There was a day when I did not think I had time for such indulgences. Now I believe they are some of the most important activities in which I participate every day.

If you want to overcome anxiety and panic, assault it from as many fronts as possible. Diet, vitamins and exercise are a powerful one-two-three punch!

5. Watch the Amount of Stress in Your Life

In the last chapter I mentioned Dave Dravecky's courageous battle with cancer. He went through a long and arduous struggle, including multiple surgeries, emotional upheaval, the loss of his arm and retirement from the sport he loved. Dave has overcome all this to minister hope to other people in dark times.

Those days were very stressful not only for him but for his wife, Jan. In the first chapter of her book *A Joy I'd Never Known* (Zondervan, 1996), Jan describes her entry into an unexpected and unwelcome season of panic and anxiety. It was brought on by an unbelievable amount of stress in her life. The list of challenges she faced within a very short time

163

was staggering, including Dave's life-and-death battle with cancer, losing her parents, moving across the country, facing national media attention and worrying about their future. Finally her system could take no more and she crashed. Thankfully Jan offered this time to the Lord and, as a result, was changed forever. Included in her transformation was a more balanced and healthy life, with an increased sensitivity to monitor her stress levels.

You, too, must be careful to limit the amount of stress in your life. After all, there is a limit to your emotional and physical stamina. Take on too much and your body will protest. Anxiety and panic are part of that rebellion. Be careful as well to monitor the number of projects you try to handle. Giving yourself breathing room, with margins of time and money and rest, are critical to your well-being. *No* must become a regular part of your vocabulary.

Some stress is unavoidable, but many times what you embrace has more to do with your drivenness than it does need. Learn to use good judgment based on sound emotional health to determine what you pick up and what you let go. That involves an internal change of attitude, which we will talk about now.

6. Release Yourself from Internal Pressure

Early in life (as we have seen) you began to avoid deep feelings of abandonment and loneliness by how you responded and related to the world around you. You grew to believe that you were responsible to do things just right and to relate to people in a certain way—and by these means to escape that scary place hidden away inside you.

Many of the attitudes and beliefs on which these actions are based are wrong and very harmful. They keep you locked in a cycle of control and striving that perpetuates fear, insecurity, anxiety and panic. We have looked at some of these faulty patterns in earlier chapters. They include:

Trying to gain acceptance through performance

People-pleasing in order to maintain a sense of connectedness

Believing you are responsible for other people's well-being

Hiding your true self in order to avoid rejection

Sacrificing your own well-being while meeting the expectations of others

Striving to achieve as compensation for your feelings of unworthiness

These patterns are extremely damaging. They lead to worry, nervousness, guilt, hypersensitivity to others, perfectionism, drivenness, indecision and, most of all, great anxiety and panic. You must reject these distorted ways of relating to others and replace them with more balanced ways of approaching your world.

To eliminate the emotional symptoms, reject the premise and replace it with truth. Central to this is learning to base your entire identity on the acceptance and intimacy that are yours in Christ Jesus. You are God's beloved child, heir to all the promises and treasures of the Kingdom. Far from alone, you have the capacity to fellowship with your heavenly Father at the very core of your being. There you can listen as He whispers words of delight and tenderness, assuring you of His unsearchable love and constant care.

These assurances will empower you to say no to any and all self-efforts to gain acceptance and approval. As a result you will relate to others not out of a need to avoid rejection but as an overflow of your unshakable relationship with God. No longer driven to perform or meet everyone's expectations, you will be free to embrace what and who the Lord directs and leave the remainder as His concern. You will no longer keep your hand closed tight in a fist, out of terrible codependency, but open it to the world. As a result you will experience peace and joy and rest where panic and anxiety once reigned over you. You will be relieving the internal pressure that keeps setting you up to say yes to external stress.

7. Learn to Be Kind to Yourself

Panic attacks can have a devastating impact on self-image. I was angry and ashamed of myself. After all, I was a pastor and Christian leader, not to mention a man! *How childish,* I told myself, *to be so afraid! What is your problem?* As I struggled with doubt, my confidence went down the chutes. Any previous notion I might have had that I was strong was annihilated. How could anyone even like me, I wondered, let alone live with me as my family did? I felt like a total loser, and at one point just wanted to crawl into a hole and die.

My negative attitude was also reflected in how I responded to my condition. I believed I was losing my mind. Whenever I got anxious I could talk myself right into a panic attack. My first reaction to fear was to think the worst and say things like, "I just can't handle this. I think I'm about to die!" My self-talk empowered the cycle of anxiety and fear. I had programmed myself to feel horrible and defeated about the entire struggle.

If you want to overcome panic, one thing you must do is change the way you feel and talk about yourself and this struggle. Positive and compassionate self-talk is part of the prescription for health. George Bernard Shaw said once that there comes a time when you have to take yourself in your own arms. That time has certainly arrived when you are declaring war on panic.

In *From Panic to Power* Lucinda Bassett gives several helpful principles for overcoming negative and destructive thinking. These include:

Admit you are a negative thinker.

Accept negative thinking as a bad habit that must be broken.

Be committed to breaking that habit.

Track your negative thoughts through the day to see how much you think that way.

Replace those thoughts with compassionate self-talk.

Be your own best friend.

Be patient with yourself.

pp. 149–153

I have also found Bassett's positive replacement statements helpful when anxiety and panic begin to arise. She encourages her readers to think:

It's no big deal.

I'm not anxious, I'm excited.

It just doesn't matter.

I'm O.K., I'll be fine.

It's just my anxiety. I'm going to float with it and it'll go away.

I'm taking this too seriously.

It's not worth getting anxious about.

I'm just tired.

Look how far I've come and the ways I've changed. So what if I still feel anxious?

pp. 155–156

Add to this list all the wonderful statements regarding God's love and care listed in chapter 5. All these truths will align your thinking with reality and produce positive, empowering feelings that rebuild confidence and the recognition that in Christ you are more than a conqueror, even when the enemies are anxiety and fear (see Romans 8:37).

8. Embrace Solitude and Stillness Disciplines

If you struggle with anxiety and panic, you are most likely an uptight person. Your world is probably very busy as you strive to juggle all the balls you have in the air at once. Your mind is flooded with thoughts most of the time and your body tense and tired. Your world could be characterized as cluttered and noisy. All of this only adds to your problem with anxiety and fear.

In his book *The Lessons of St. Francis* (Dutton, 1997), artist and author John Michael Talbot writes:

> In many ways, our lives are a lot like ponds. When things are calm, you can see clear down to the bottom, and detect the slightest movement and motion. But when things are unsettled, everything's murky and impenetrable. Unfortunately, few of us have lives that are like a still, serene pond. For most of us, life is more like a kitchen blender, its engine humming, its blades purring, and its motion making a puree of the elements of our fast-paced, turbulent lives.
>
> pp. 55–56

How does this description fit your life? If you battle anxiety and panic, it is probably quite accurate. If so, consider bringing change into your schedule in order to silence the noise and remove the clutter that is smothering you. The time has come for space in your life for rest and relaxation.

Embrace solitude and silence as spiritual disciplines. They will help you unload the burdens of life while filling your body, mind and spirit with renewed strength and spiritual vitality. Granted, it is not easy to break those old habits of busyness and the patterns that keep your world in constant motion. But you must clear out such space if you want to overcome the fear that has you locked in panic and anxiety.

After a while you will find it essential to guard time each day for solitude and silence. If possible slip away to a special place and sit. Focus your mind on something pleasant and positive, particularly centering on the presence of God in the moment. Contemplate His great love and imagine Him there sitting with you. Try not to pray or read during this time. Rather, practice communion with the Lord in a spirit of rest. It can be beneficial to learn some relaxation techniques that will help you unwind the tension that has built up in your body. When possible listen to music, particularly instrumental, that refreshes your emotional reserves.

The more time you can spend in moments like this, the more discerning and productive you will be when moving back into the activity of your world. Remember, embracing solitude and silence takes discipline. Many tasks and people call for your time. So make quiet time a nonnegotiable daily part of your life. Occasionally spend an entire day or weekend in solitude and silence as a special gift to yourself. I assure you, over time such seasons apart will become treasures to your life, enabling you to walk in greater peace and rest.

9. Learn to Let It Pass

The worst thing you can ever do is listen to what irrational panic is telling you to do. On the one hand panic is a natural response to a real threat, sending a message for you to either get out of the situation or fight against your enemy. But when normal panic moves to panic disorder, your emotions are engaging even though there is no real threat. Everything within you feels as if your life is in danger, so you react in fear and flight.

I know how strong the urge to run in response to panic attacks can be. For a long time I did run, conditioning myself to believe there really was a threat. I have mentioned that I avoided many places because I did not want to experience panic. But instead of winning by that method, I invited increased bondage. So stand your ground when anxiety and panic try to take over. Don't try to manage it or obey the urge to run. Be honest, telling yourself that it is happening, and then just let it pass.

Imagine that panic is a cloud temporarily passing over you. The sun will come out again; just be patient. Tell yourself everything is O.K., that you will survive and that you will be fine. Ask the Lord for self-control and don't do the things you did previously in reaction. Use positive self-talk and move right through it. By doing these things you are calling panic a liar and standing on the truth of God's Word and His ability to see you through to the other side.

I have a friend who owns a yacht and often sails the ocean on long voyages. The best thing to do in stormy seas, he tells me, is to aim right into the waves and keep moving ahead. To do otherwise would risk true disaster, even though the natural instinct is to turn away from it.

You must do the same with your panic. Once you have done what I have suggested in the eight previous steps, face panic when it comes and ride it out.

Then, on the other side, don't get down on yourself that you had an attack. Pat yourself on the back that you handled it well and give yourself some reward for a job well done. Later ask the Lord to show you what was going on— why panic came on as it did. You will find that fatigue, a negative thought, the buildup of stress or some other factor empowered the anxiety. Now make the necessary adjustments and move on with confidence.

10. Choose Your Battles Wisely

Finally, be sure you are using wisdom about conquering your fears. Most likely you have avoided places that induced fear and panic in your life, possibly to the point of significantly limiting your world. As you move toward freedom, you will want to reclaim the ground you gave away because of your struggle. This is a healthy goal. But be sure you develop a strategy that will help you win.

If you stopped driving because of panic, for example, it may not be helpful to decide that you are going to beat it now by driving alone on the first day in New York's rush hour. That is a difficult task for anyone and could well set you back.

Instead, make a list of all the places panic has taken from you. Rank them in order according to your desire to overcome them. Once you have done this, begin with what you ranked highest and set a strategy to reclaim the activity.

Let's use the driving illustration again. You might decide that your first trip will be a brief one in the daylight with a friend along as support. From there take measured steps to increase your confidence. Maybe the next time you will take that short daylight trip alone, followed by any one of countless options that you feel ready to face. The point is, use wisdom and give yourself the best possible chance to win. Soon you will be driving with little thought about it, confident and at peace, having taken back an important part of your life.

Use the same strategy for other activities, and over time you will be enjoying life as God intended. When you have a setback, accept it and determine what brought on the anxiety, learning from the experience. Remember, this is built on

171

all the steps we have discussed in this book. The practical suggestions I lay out in this chapter are effective only when you have addressed the deeper issues in your life. Once you allow God to go to the core issues, these steps and techniques become tools empowered by His presence for your freedom.

An Ending That Promises a New Beginning

You *can* begin to overcome the fear that has held you captive for so long! God is ready to meet you in the darkness and transform it into a place of peace. Go there with Him, experience His presence and listen to His whispers of love and devotion. His love is unconditional, it is lavish, it is perfect. Allow Him to touch you with its transforming power and you will know that John was right. Perfect love does drive away fear, and in its place come contentment and rest. You will be able to face life and its challenges with new strength, regardless of the level of risk, knowing that your heavenly Father is right there, committed at all times to your very best.

As one fellow traveler to another, I encourage you to position yourself for freedom by doing the work we have talked about in this book. Allow the Lord to address the core wounds of your life, admitting openly that you are battling fear. Go to that dark place with Him and renounce every false premise that keeps you locked in bondage. Say yes to His work, even when it involves a season in the desert where you will learn to say no to the distractions and painkillers that keep you from the freedom the Lord intends for you. Discover the transforming power of your Father's incomparable love and let that divine affection flow into your relationships with other people. To help, learn to *T-r-u-s-t*, just as we discussed, and when panic threatens, follow the ten steps I have shared in this chapter.

As you prepare to move forward, meditate on these words from God found in Isaiah 41:13–14. They are a promise that will strengthen you to journey into the darkness of your own fears and beyond to the place of His glorious embrace. I pray that this passage will empower you to take yet another step forward toward freedom and peace in Him. His hand is extended toward you as He speaks these words:

> "I am the LORD, your God, who takes hold of your right hand and says to you, Do not fear; I will help you. Do not be afraid . . . for I myself will help you."

You are far from alone and abandoned! The Lord God is right there with you, even as you read these words. Turn to Him and I assure you that something far more powerful than fear will well up within your heart. You will feel the new beginning of a glorious reconnection with the One who loves you. And you will find the strength of His peace that He designed, from the first moment of time, just for you.

Questions for Reflection and Review

1. In what way can panic disorder positively affect your relationship with the Lord?

2. What is the relationship between panic attacks and your thinking patterns?

3. Is there any connection between your core woundings and panic attacks? If so, what do you think it is and why?

4. How can the evil one work against you in this problem? What can you do to combat his schemes?

5. What reasons are there for receiving a medical checkup as part of your strategy to overcome panic attacks?

173

6. To what degree are you watching your intake of sugar, caffeine and coffee? What can you do to reduce these items from your diet? Why is this important?

7. What is the relationship between stress and panic? What changes can you make in your life to address this issue?

8. Reread the section entitled "Release Yourself from Internal Pressure." Where are you caught in faulty patterns? What will you do about it?

9. What is compassionate self-talk? How does that affect panic and anxiety?

10. In what ways have you scheduled time for silence and relaxation in your day?

11. What do I mean when I encourage you to learn to let panic attacks pass?

12. Why is it important that you choose your battles wisely? Select a place where you want to reclaim ground taken by panic. What is your strategy?

Selected Bibliography

Bassett, Lucinda. *From Panic to Power.* New York: HarperCollins, 1995.

Bernard of Clairvaux. *The Love of God.* Portland: Multnomah, 1983.

Brother Lawrence. *The Practice of the Presence of God.* New York: Doubleday, 1977.

de Caussade, Jean Pierre. *The Sacrament of the Present Moment.* New York: HarperCollins, 1989.

Crabb, Larry. *Connecting: A Radical New Vision.* Nashville: Word, 1997.

Dravecky, David. *Comeback.* Grand Rapids: Zondervan / HarperSanFrancisco, 1990.

———. *When You Can't Come Back.* Grand Rapids: Zondervan / HarperSanFrancisco, 1994.

Dravecky, Jan. *A Joy I'd Never Known.* Grand Rapids: Zondervan, 1996.

Fénelon, François. *The Seeking Heart.* Beaumont, Tex.: Seed Sowers, 1992.

———. *Let Go.* Springdale, Pa.: Whitaker House, 1973.

Fitz-Gibbon, Andy and Jane Fitz-Gibbon. *The Kiss of Intimacy.* Crowborough, U.K.: Monarch, 1995.

Gire, Kenneth. *Windows of the Soul.* Grand Rapids: Zondervan, 1996.

Guyon, Jeanne. *Experiencing the Depths of Jesus Christ.* Beaumont, Tex.: Seed Sowers, 1975.

Hallesby, Ole. *Prayer.* Minneapolis: Augsburg / Fortress, 1994.

Kelly, Thomas R. *A Testament of Devotion.* New York: HarperCollins, 1992.

Mulholland, Robert. *Invitation to a Journey: A Road Map for Spiritual Formation.* Downers Grove, Ill.: InterVarsity Press, 1992.

Nouwen, Henri J. M. *Making All Things New.* New York: HarperCollins, 1981.

———. *Lifesigns: Intimacy, Fecundity, and Ecstasy in Christian Perspective.* New York: Doubleday/Image, 1990.

———. *Return of the Prodigal Son.* Doubleday/Image, 1994.

———. *The Inner Voice of Love.* New York: Doubleday, 1996.

———. *Reaching Out: Three Movements of the Spiritual Life.* New York: Doubleday/Image, 1986.

Saint John of the Cross. *Dark Night of the Soul.* New York: Doubleday/Image, 1990.

Smith, James Bryan. *Embracing the Love of God.* San Francisco: HarperSanFrancisco, 1995.

Tozer, A. W. *The Pursuit of God.* Camp Hill, Pa.: Christian Publications, 1982.

Wardle, Terry. *Draw Close to the Fire.* Grand Rapids: Chosen, 1998.